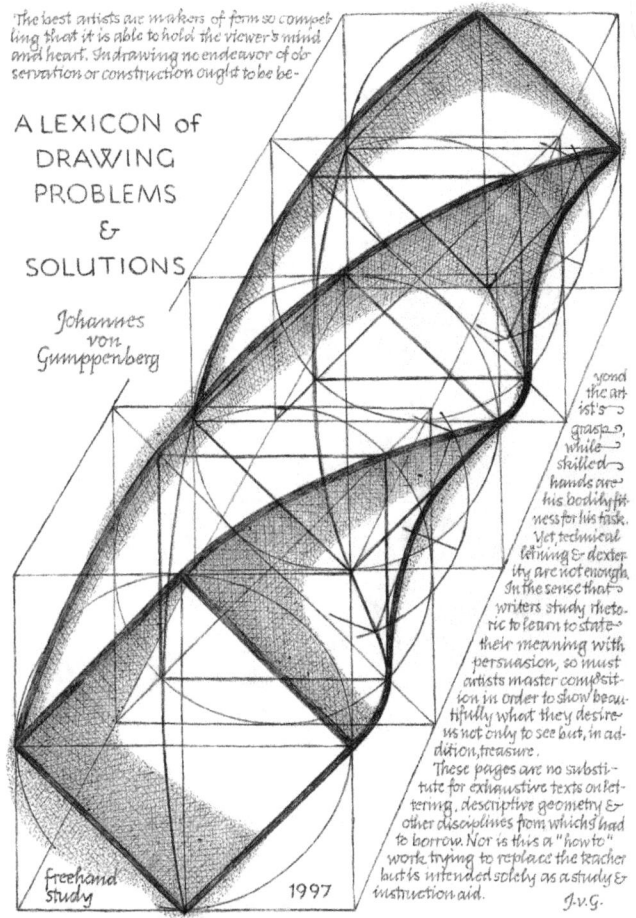

The best artists are makers of form so compelling that it is able to hold the viewer's mind and heart. In drawing no endeavor of observation or construction ought to be be-

A LEXICON of
DRAWING
PROBLEMS
&
SOLUTIONS

Johannes
von
Gumppenberg

yond the artist's grasp, while skilled hands are his bodily fitness for his task. Yet technical lettering & dexterity are not enough. In the sense that writers study rhetoric to learn to state their meaning with persuasion, so must artists master composition in order to show beautifully what they desire us not only to see but, in addition, treasure.

These pages are no substitute for exhaustive texts on lettering, descriptive geometry & other disciplines from which I had to borrow. Nor is this a "how to" work trying to replace the teacher but is intended solely as a study & instruction aid.

J.v.G.

freehand
study

1997

# A Lexicon of Drawing
# Problems and Solutions

Johannes H. von Gumppenberg

For Janet: No worker in whatever calling may hope for a
more gracious gift than lucid understanding joined with love.

PLATE 1

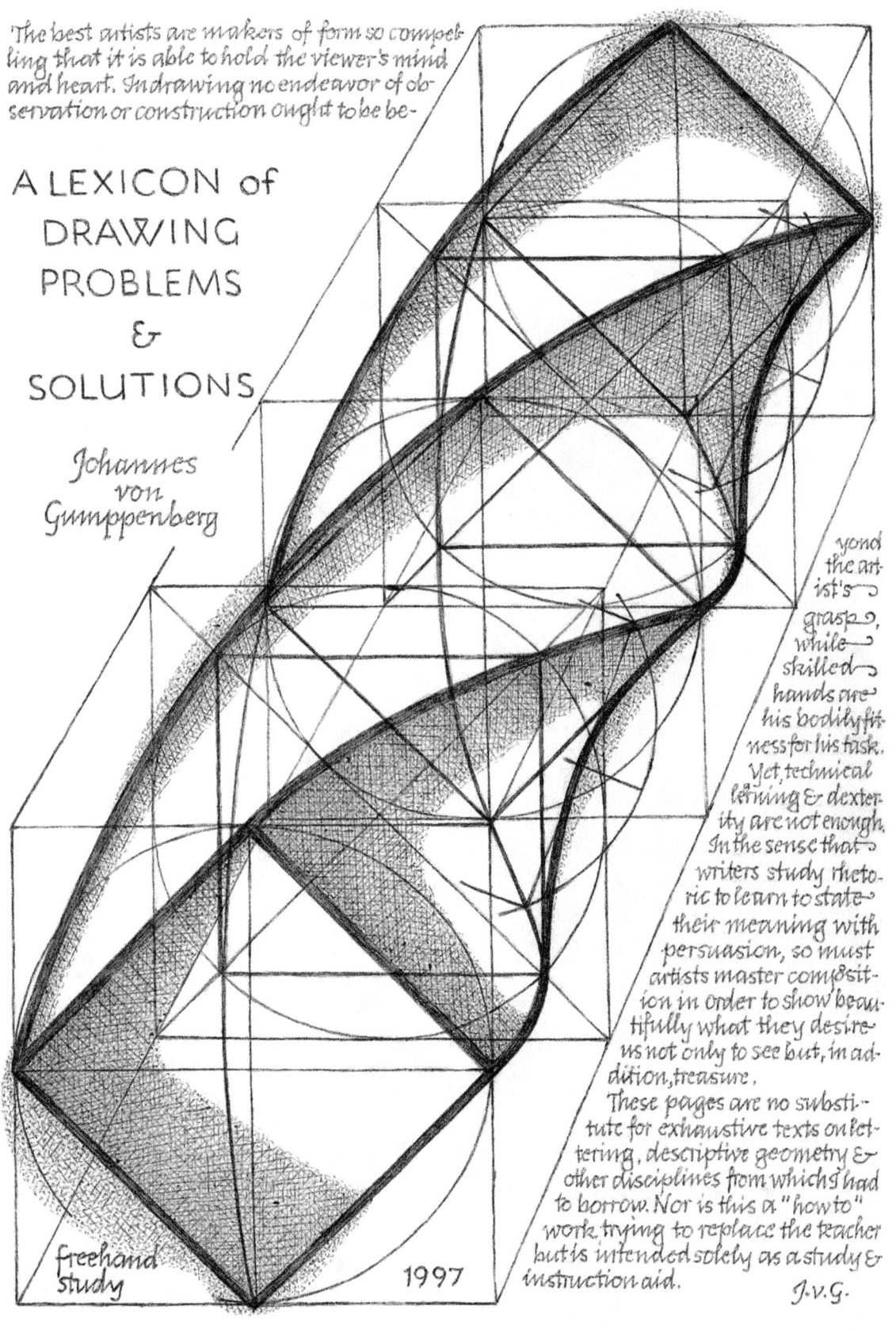

The best artists are makers of form so compelling that it is able to hold the viewer's mind and heart. In drawing no endeavor of observation or construction ought to be be-

# A LEXICON of
# DRAWING
# PROBLEMS
# &
# SOLUTIONS

Johannes
von
Gumppenberg

-yond the artist's grasp, while skilled hands are his bodily fitness for his task. Yet technical learning & dexterity are not enough. In the sense that writers study rhetoric to learn to state their meaning with persuasion, so must artists master composition in order to show beautifully what they desire us not only to see but, in addition, treasure.

These pages are no substitute for exhaustive texts on lettering, descriptive geometry & other disciplines from which I had to borrow. Nor is this a "how to" work, trying to replace the teacher but is intended solely as a study & instruction aid.

J.v.G.

freehand
study

1997

PLATE 2

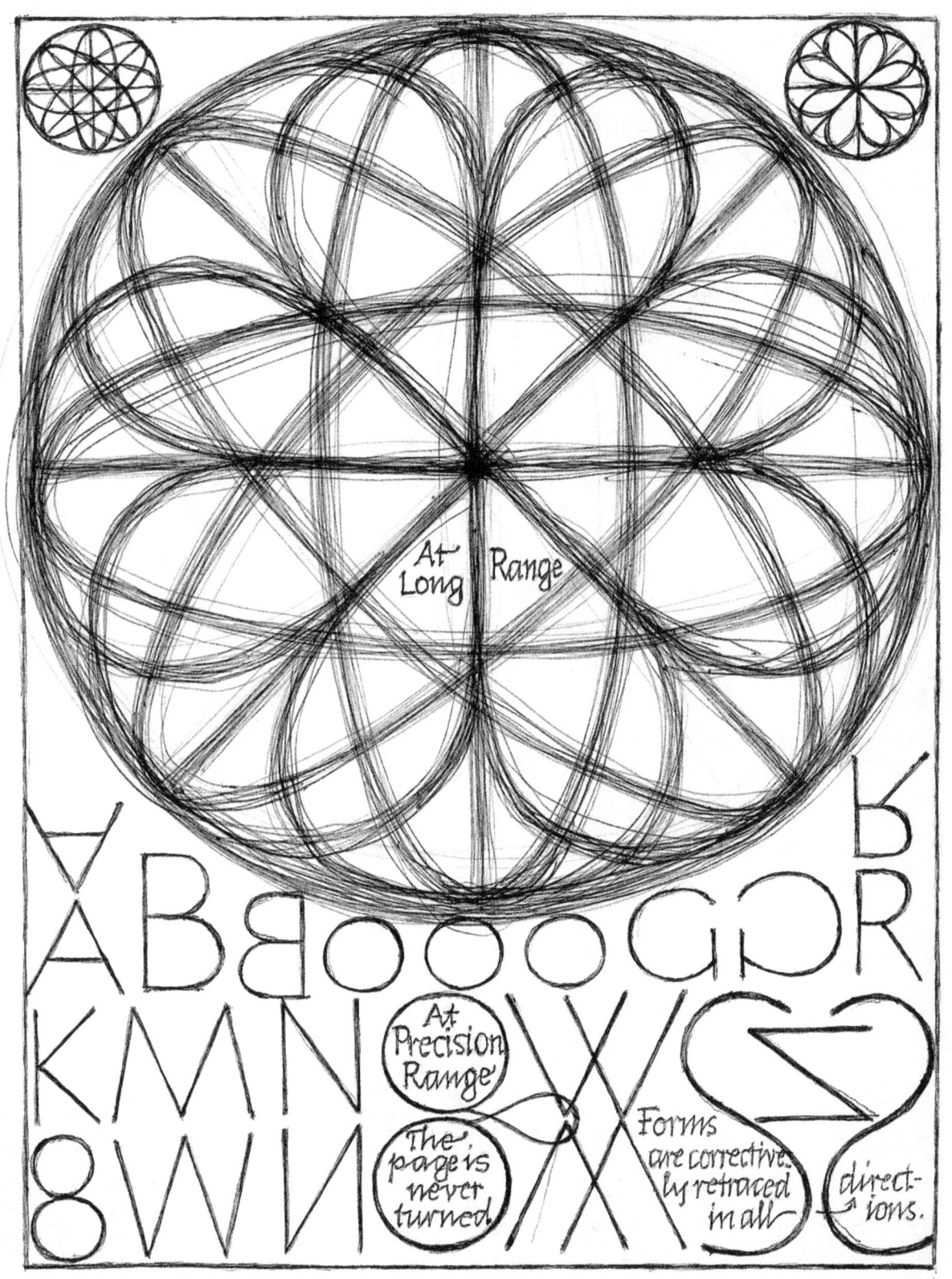

At Long Range

At Precision Range

The page is never turned

Forms are correctively retraced in all directions.

DEXTERITY TRAINING

J·G·1995

PLATE 3

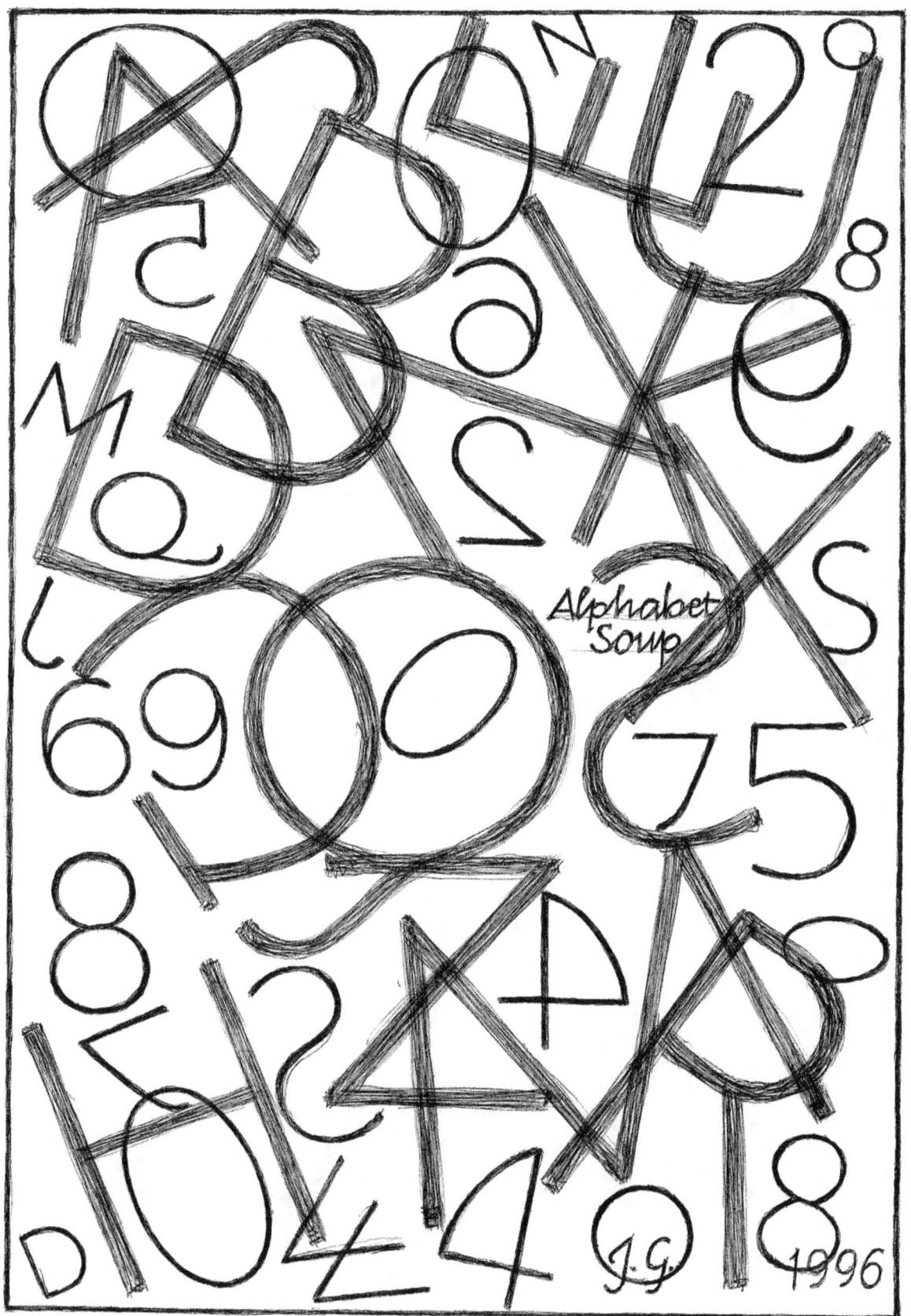

Alphabet Soup

J.G.

1996

PLATE 4

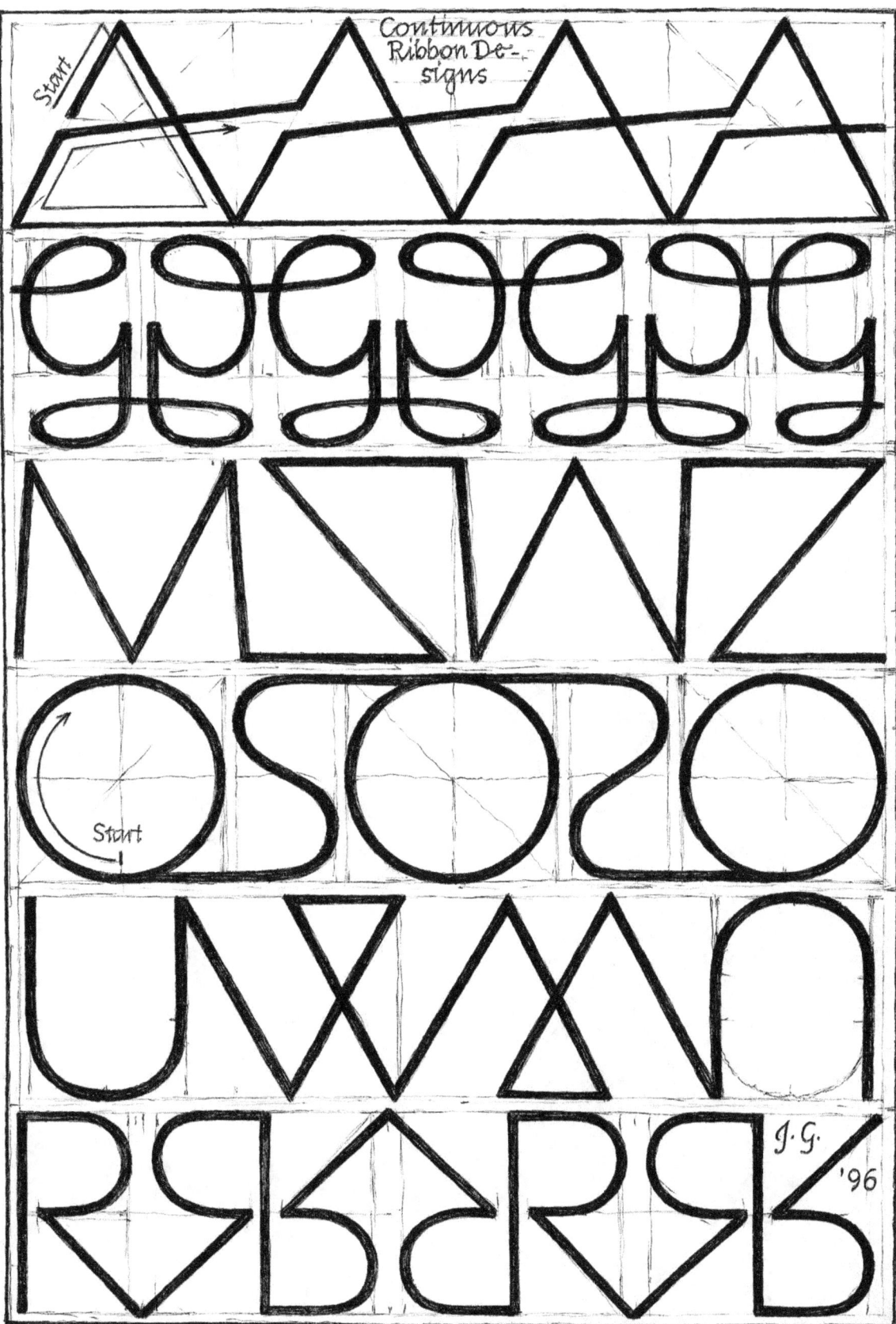

Continuous Ribbon De-signs

Start

Start

J.G.
'96

PLATE 5

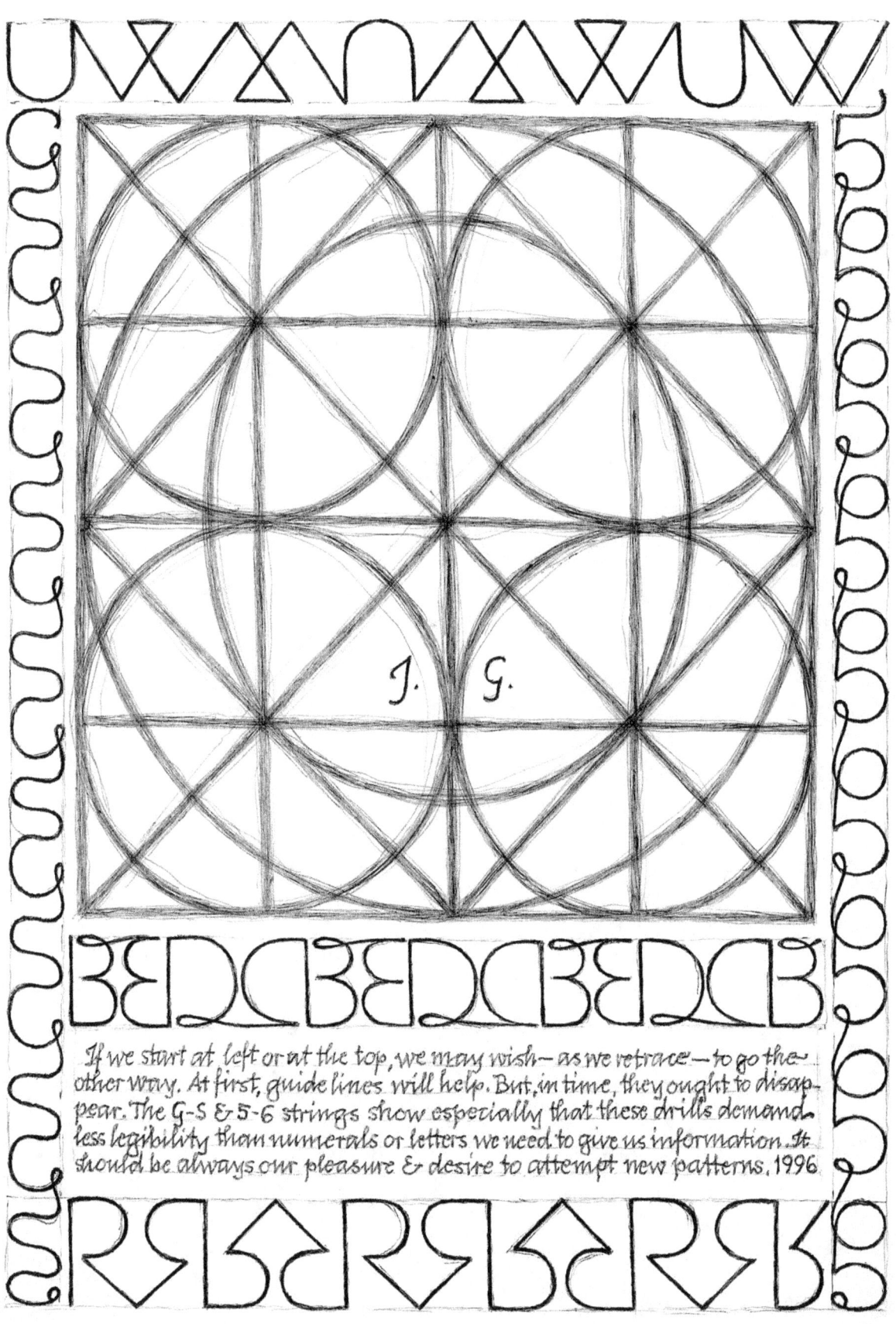

J. G.

If we start at left or at the top, we may wish — as we retrace — to go the other way. At first, guide lines will help. But, in time, they ought to disappear. The G-S & 5-6 strings show especially that these drills demand less legibility than numerals or letters we need to give us information. It should be always our pleasure & desire to attempt new patterns. 1996

PLATE 6

Skill Exercises reveal weaknesses,— mine are pushing level lines, obliques & the corresponding curves from <u>Right to left</u>. As, drawn that way, preceding shapes are likely covered by the Hand & cannot serve as samples for their followers, light linear guides at for the first attempts almost indispensible. Proceed from right to left; then retrace—beginning at the finish & ending at the start.

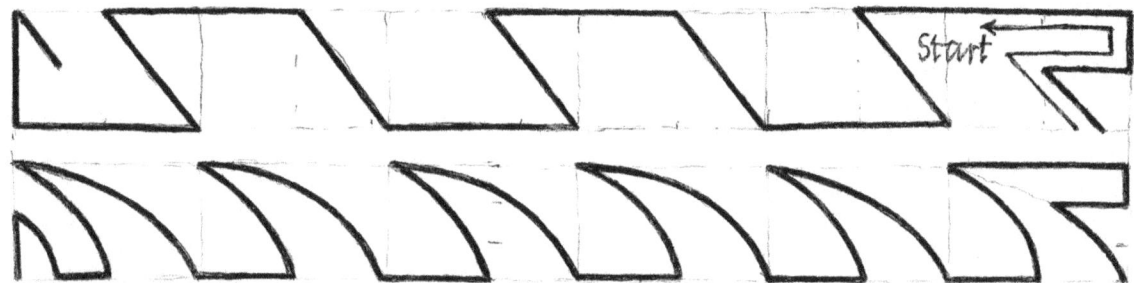

Start

Traversing all the page, draw lines in every combination and direct-ion, particularly those you find uncomfortable to pursue. Then re-shape them—still in all directions & without any rotation of the page— till a co-herent, powerful design results & yields a harvest of new shapes.

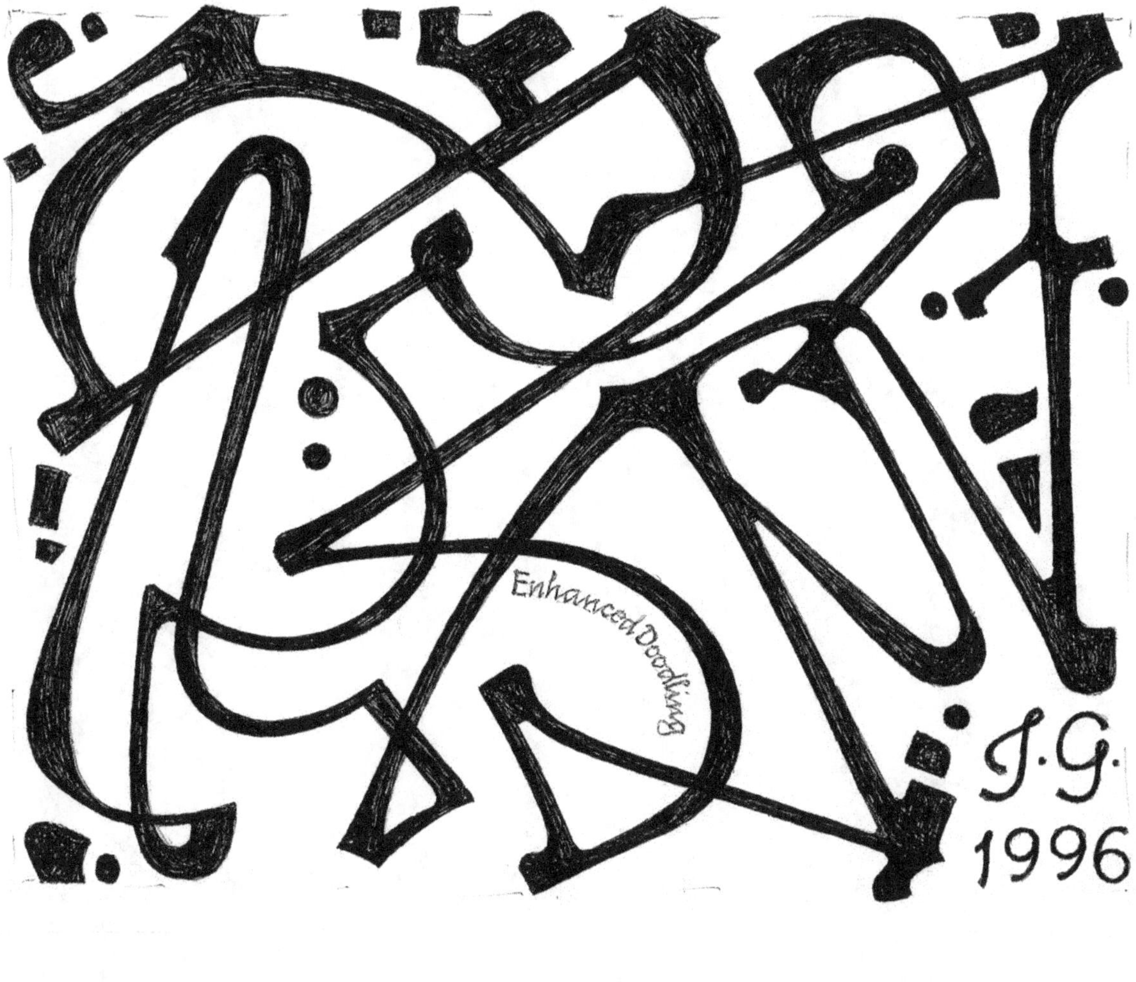

Enhanced Doodling

J·G·
1996

PLATE 7

**DEXTERITY**
*Training*

J.G. 1996

PLATE 8

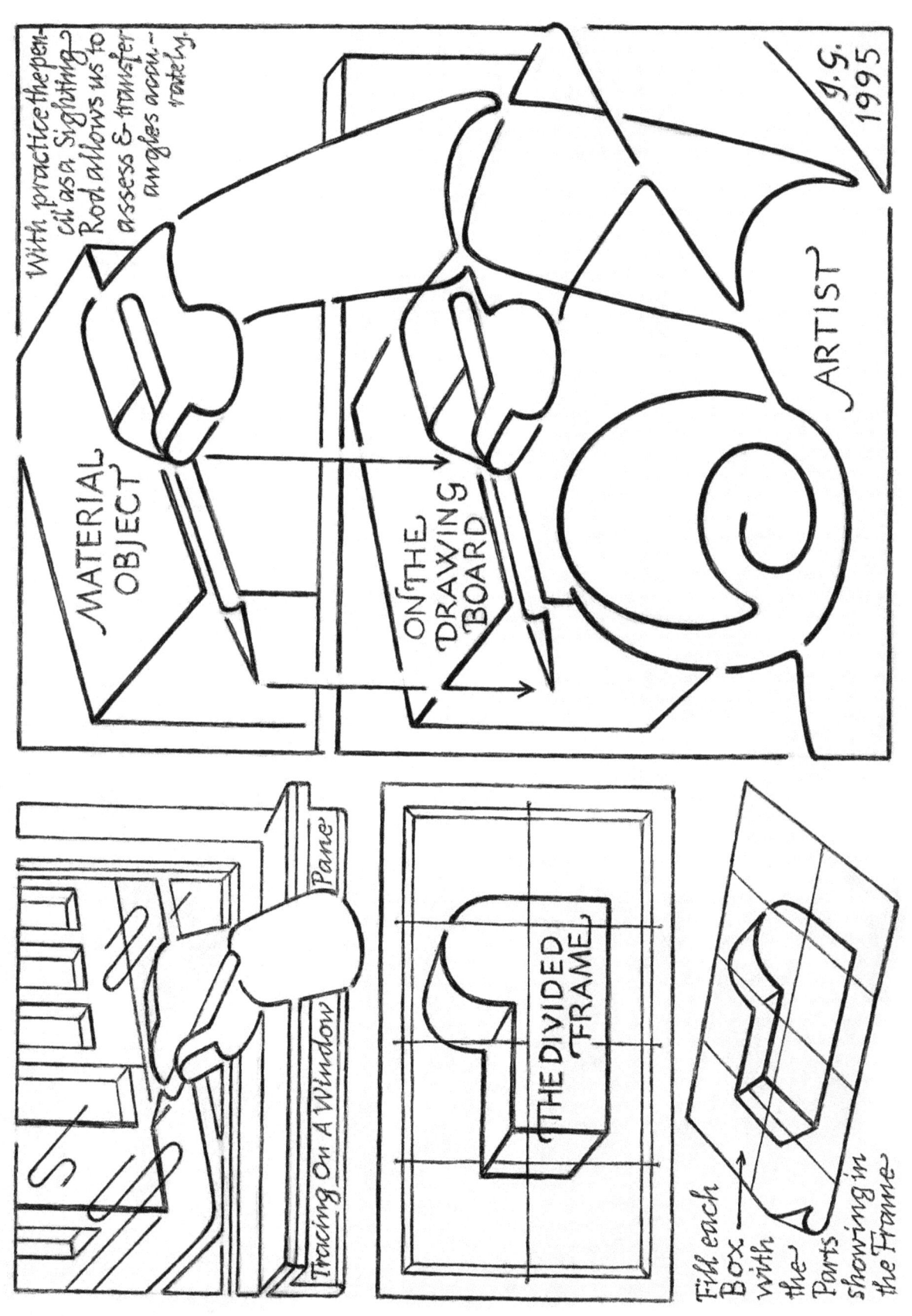

PLATE 9

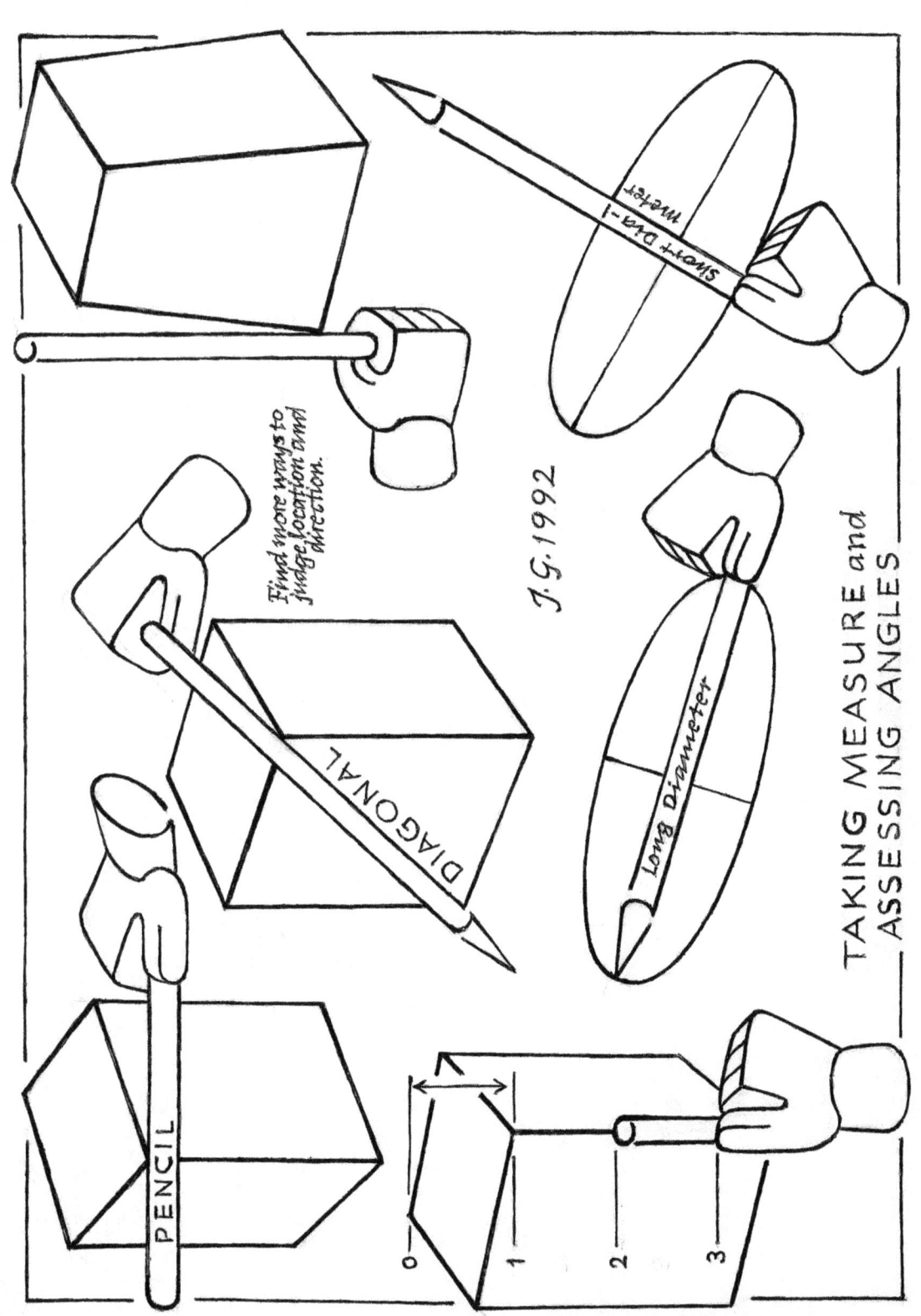

Find more ways to judge location and direction.

J.G. 1992

Short Dia-1 meter

Long Diameter

DIAGONAL

PENCIL

0 1 2 3

TAKING MEASURE and ASSESSING ANGLES

PLATE 10

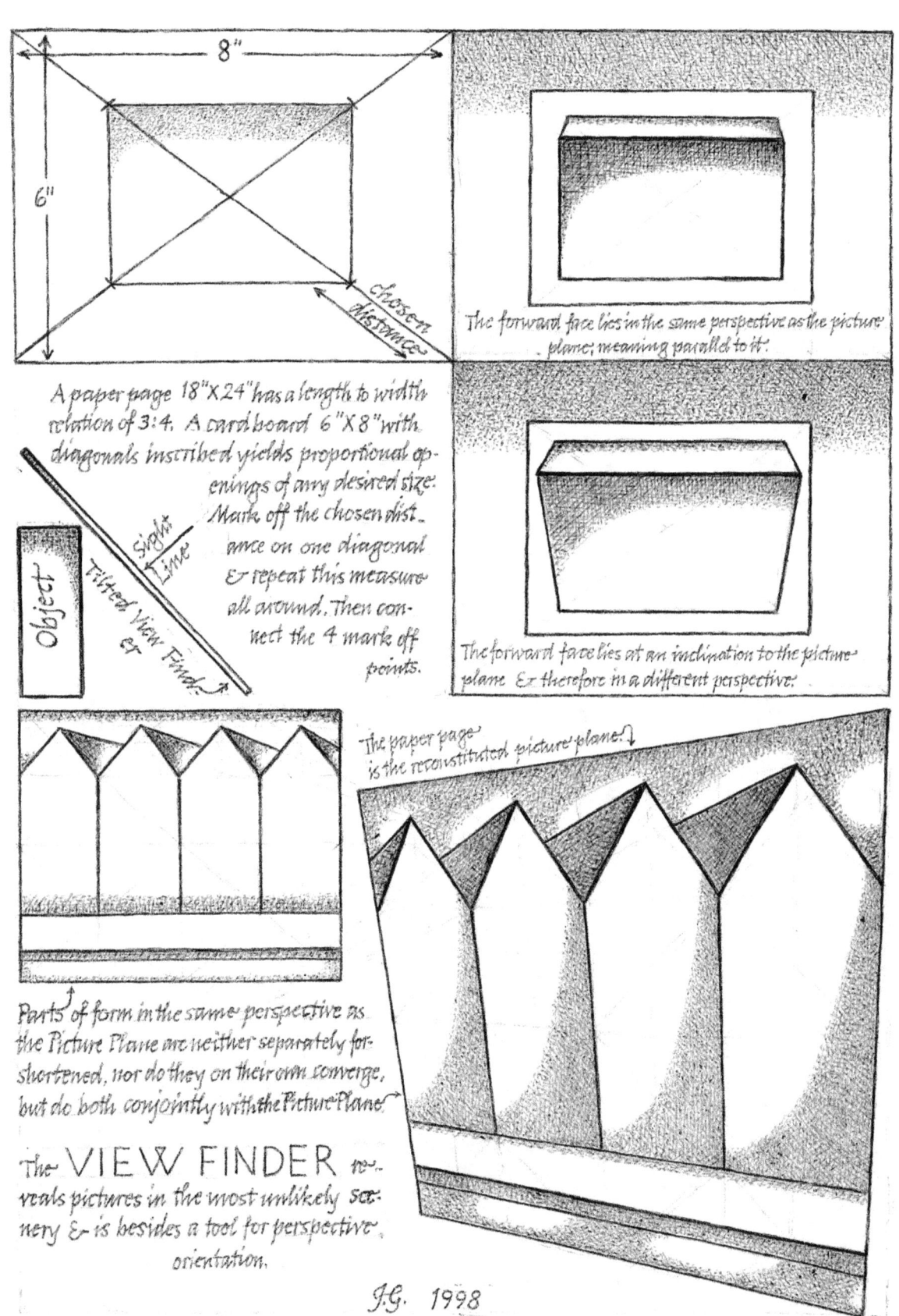

8"

6"

*chosen distance*

*Object*

*Tilted View Finder*

*Sight Line*

A paper page 18"×24" has a length to width relation of 3:4. A cardboard 6"×8" with diagonals inscribed yields proportional openings of any desired size. Mark off the chosen dist-ance on one diagonal & repeat this measure all around. Then con-nect the 4 mark off points.

The forward face lies in the same perspective as the picture plane; meaning parallel to it.

The forward face lies at an inclination to the picture plane & therefore in a different perspective.

The paper page is the reconstituted picture plane.

Parts of form in the same perspective as the Picture Plane are neither separately for-shortened, nor do they on their own converge, but do both conjointly with the Picture Plane.

The VIEW FINDER re-veals pictures in the most unlikely scen-nery &- is besides a tool for perspective orientation.

J.G. 1998

*PLATE 11*

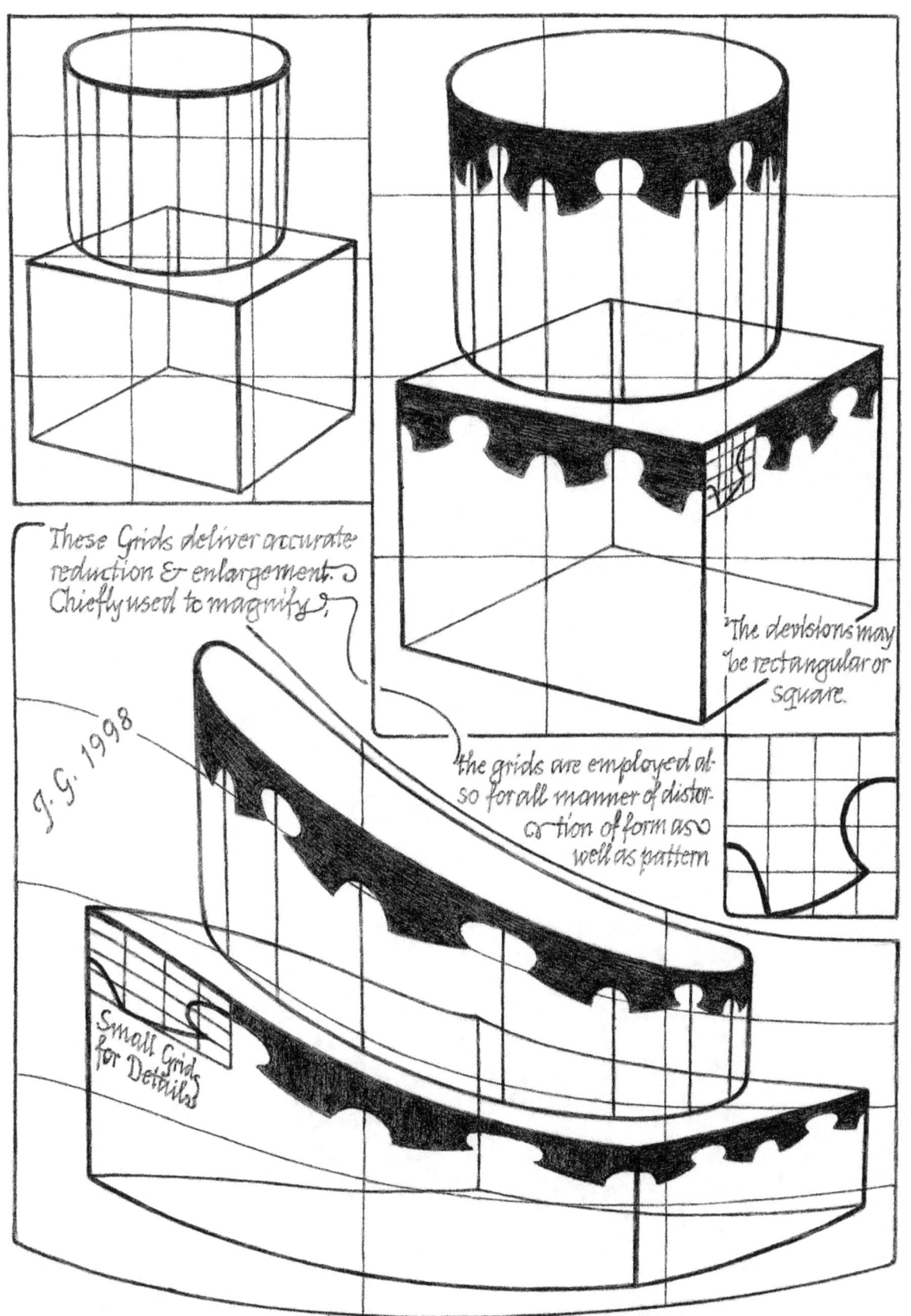

These Grids deliver accurate
reduction & enlargement.
Chiefly used to magnify,

J. G. 1998

The devisions may
be rectangular or
square.

the grids are employed also for all manner of distor-
tion of form as
well as pattern

Small Grids
for Details

PLATE 12

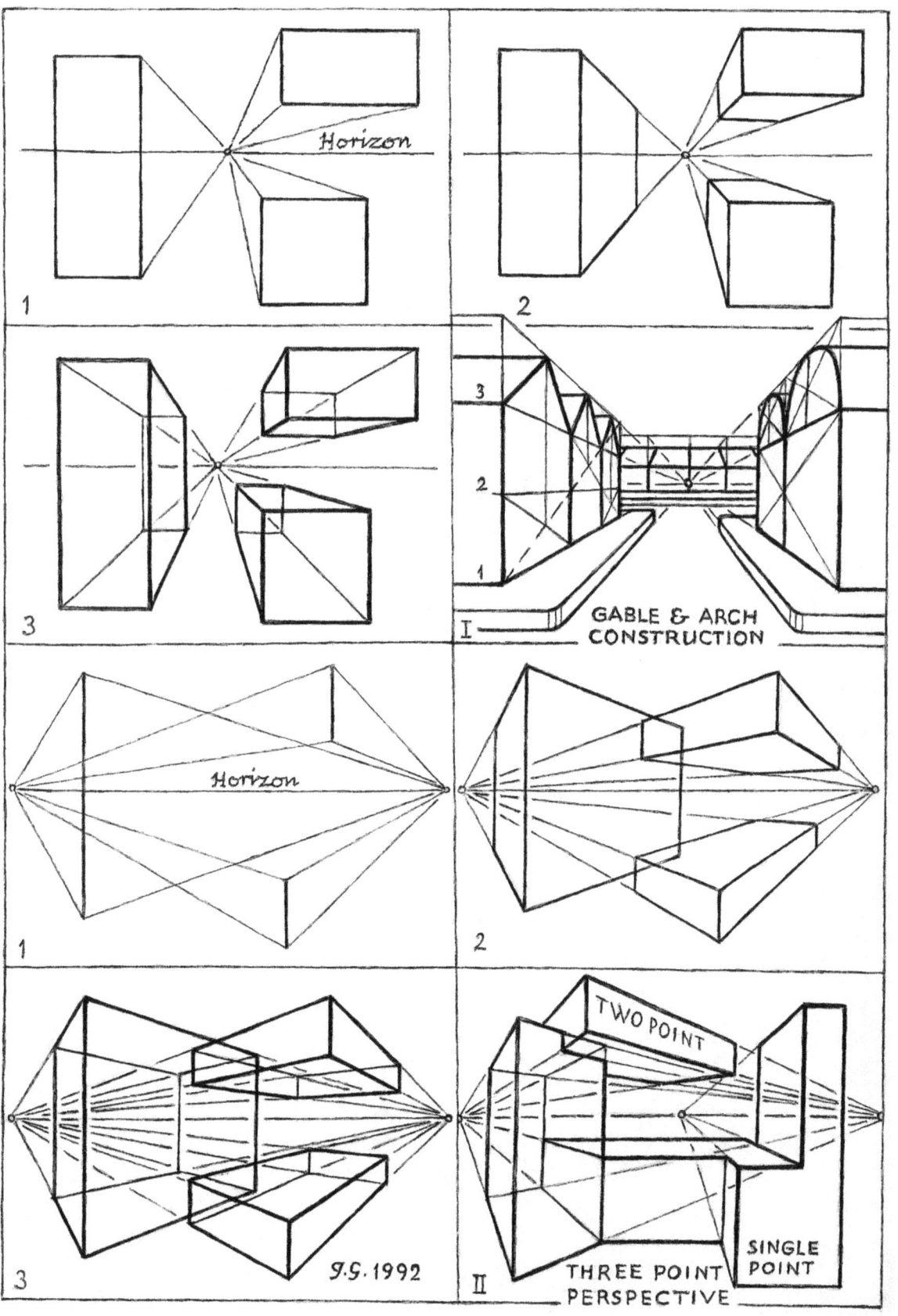

1

2

Horizon

3

I    GABLE & ARCH
CONSTRUCTION

1    Horizon

2

3    J.G. 1992

TWO POINT

THREE POINT
PERSPECTIVE

SINGLE
POINT

II

PLATE 13

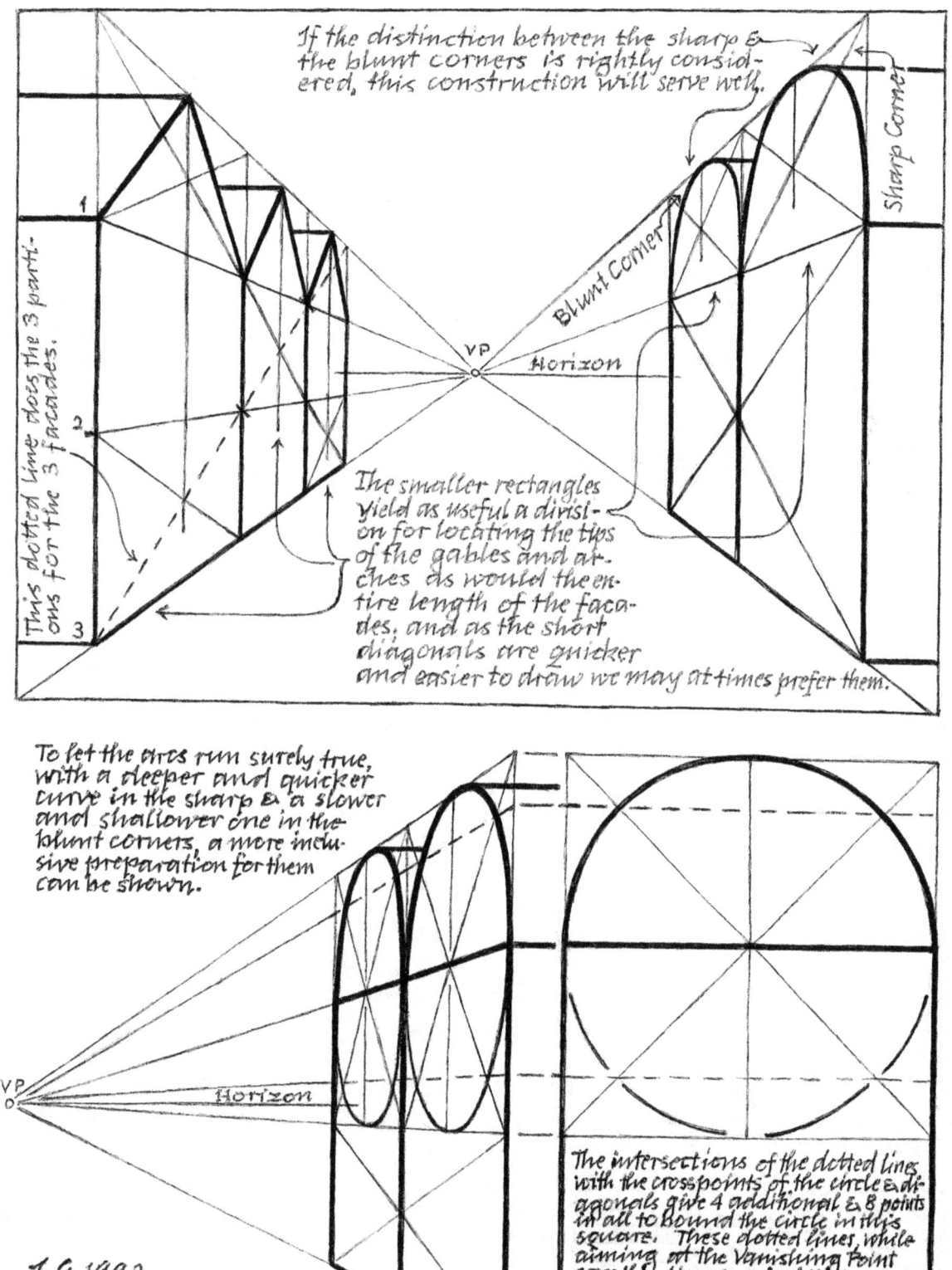

If the distinction between the sharp & the blunt corners is rightly considered, this construction will serve well.

*Sharp Corner*

*Blunt Corner*

VP

Horizon

This dotted line does the 3 partitions for the 3 facades.

1

2

3

The smaller rectangles yield as useful a division for locating the tips of the gables and arches as would the entire length of the facades, and as the short diagonals are quicker and easier to draw we may at times prefer them.

To let the arcs run surely true, with a deeper and quicker curve in the sharp & a slower and shallower one in the blunt corners, a more inclusive preparation for them can be shown.

VP

Horizon

J·G·1992

The intersections of the dotted lines with the crosspoints of the circle & diagonals give 4 additional & 8 points in all to bound the circle in this square. These dotted lines, while aiming at the vanishing point cross the diagonals of the two perspective squares at points the fore-shortened (elliptical) circular arcs at left must also traverse.

PLATE 14

# FLYING FORMS

We are used to level arrangements of objects whose vanishing points fall upon the visible horizon. Yet, if you fling one of the solids on the right leaping & tumbling into space, it will throughout assume numerous perspectives — all of them correct & true; and these perspectives will then accord with vanishing traces whose tilting angles always alter.

As these arrays turn around a central vanishing point, the forms appear to be rather more afloat in space than rolling?

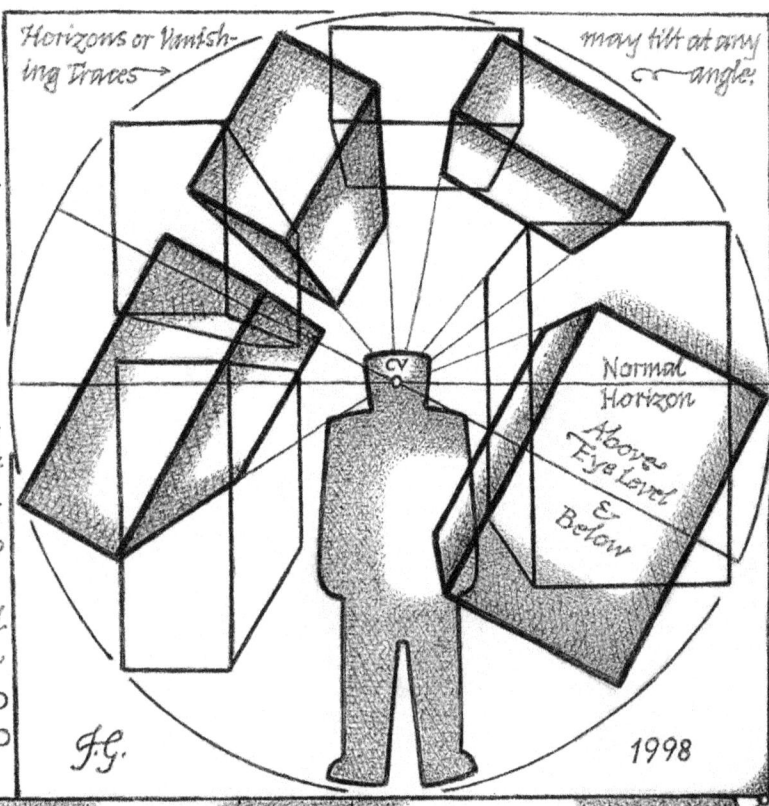

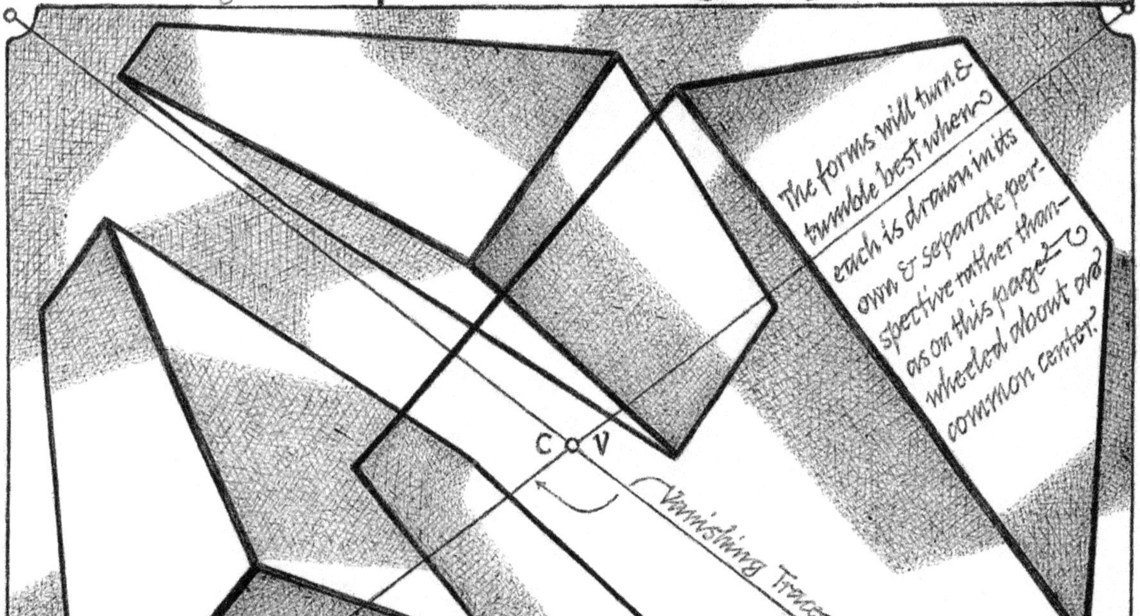

Horizons or Vanishing Traces →

may tilt at any angle.

CV

Normal Horizon

Above Eye Level & Below

J.G.

1998

The forms will turn & tumble best when each is drawn in its own & separate perspective rather than as on this page — wheeled about a common center.

C ○ V

← Vanishing Traces

PLATE 15

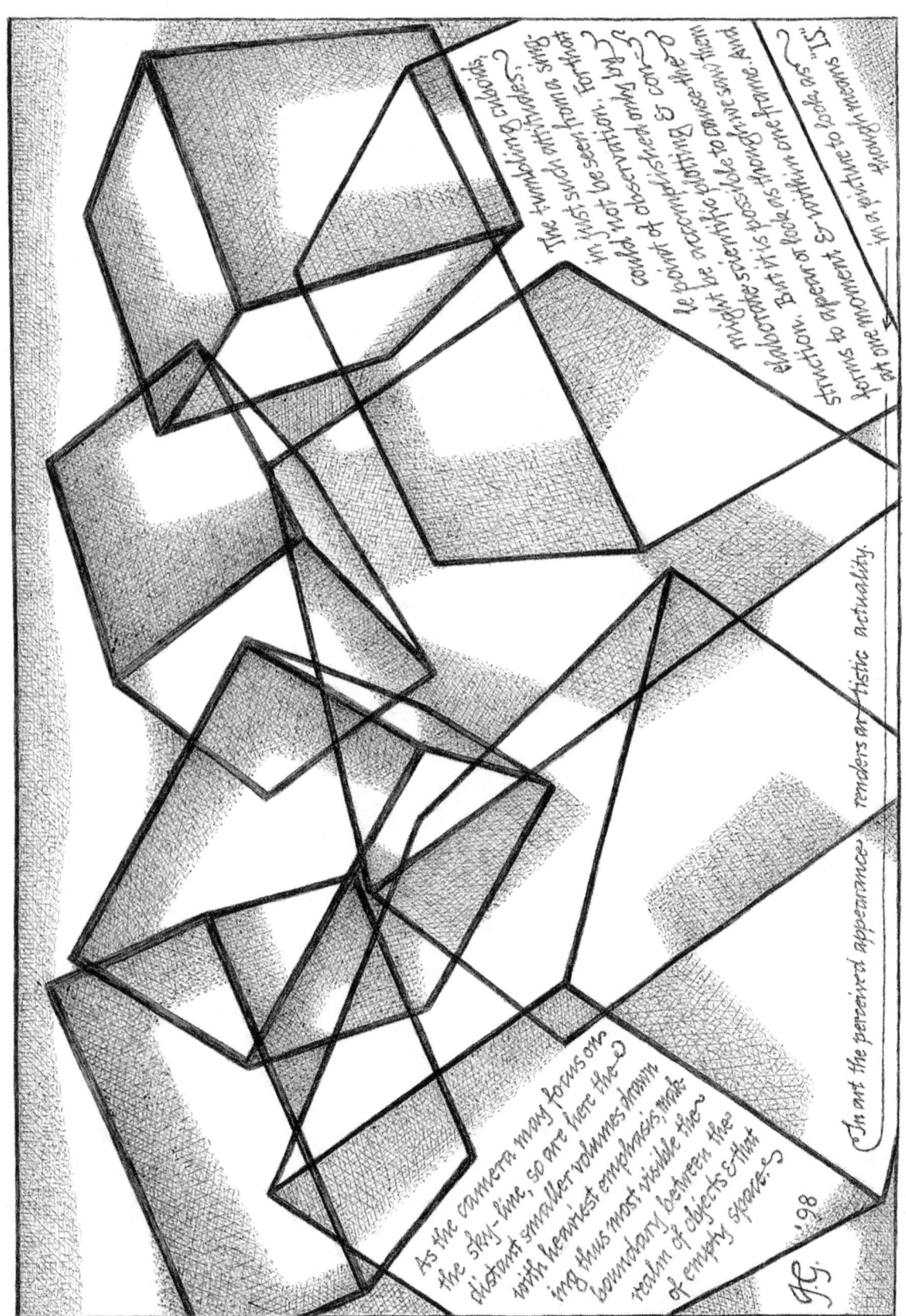

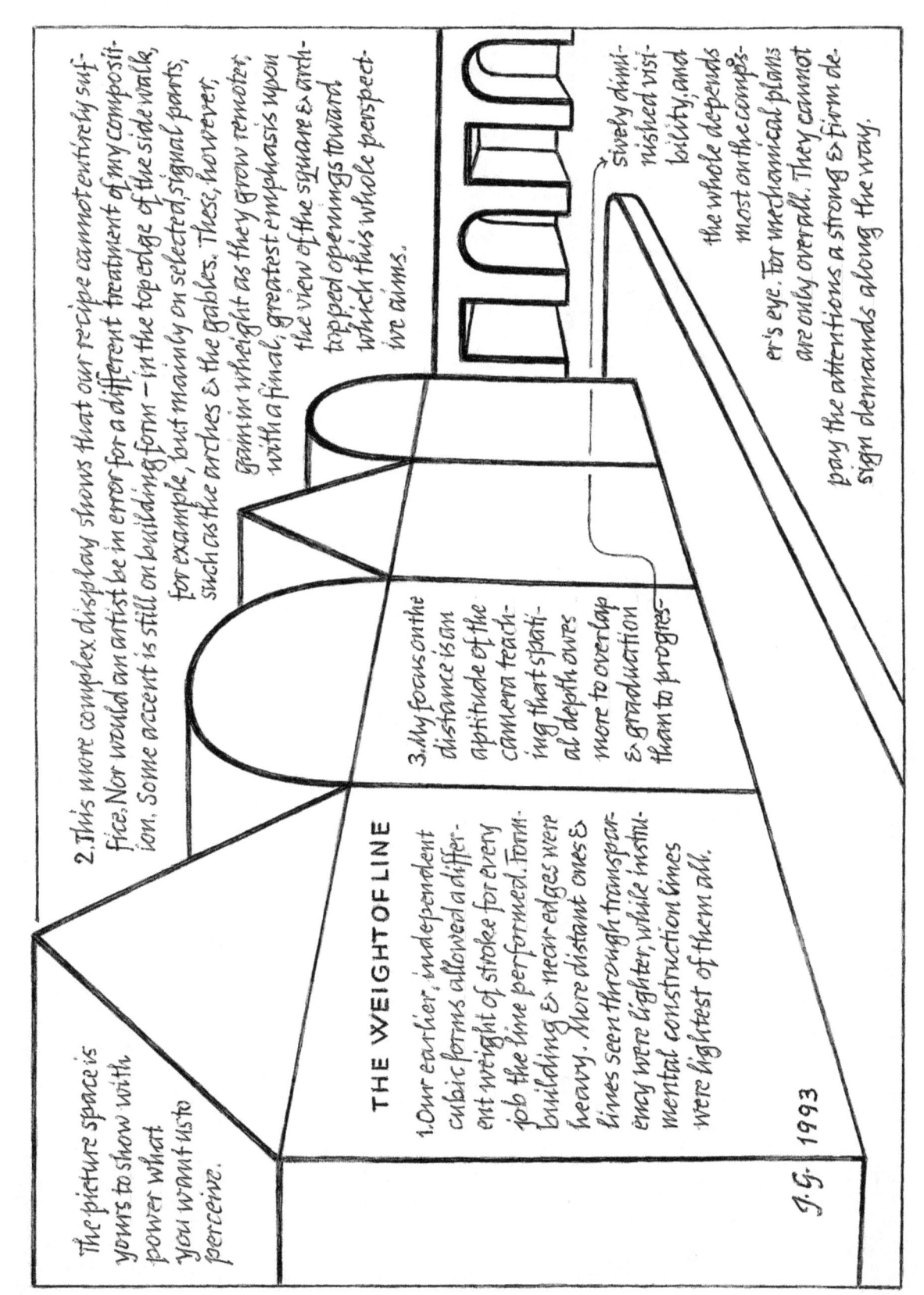

The picture space is yours to show with power what you want us to perceive.

## THE WEIGHT OF LINE

1. Our earlier, independent cubic forms allowed a different weight of stroke for every job the line performed. Form-building & near edges were heavy. More distant ones & lines seen through transparency were lighter, while instrumental construction lines were lightest of them all.

3. My focus on the distance is an aptitude of the camera teaching that spatial depth owes more to overlap & graduation than to progres-

2. This more complex display shows that our recipe cannot entirely suffice. Nor would an artist be in error for a different treatment of my composition. Some accent is still on building form – in the top edge of the sidewalk, for example, but mainly on selected, signal parts, such as the arches & the gables. These, however, gain in weight as they grow remoter, with a final, greatest emphasis upon the view of the square & arch-topped openings toward which this whole perspective aims.

sively diminished visibility, and the whole depends most on the composer's eye. For mechanical plans are only overall. They cannot pay the attentions a strong & firm design demands along the way.

J.G. 1993

PLATE 17

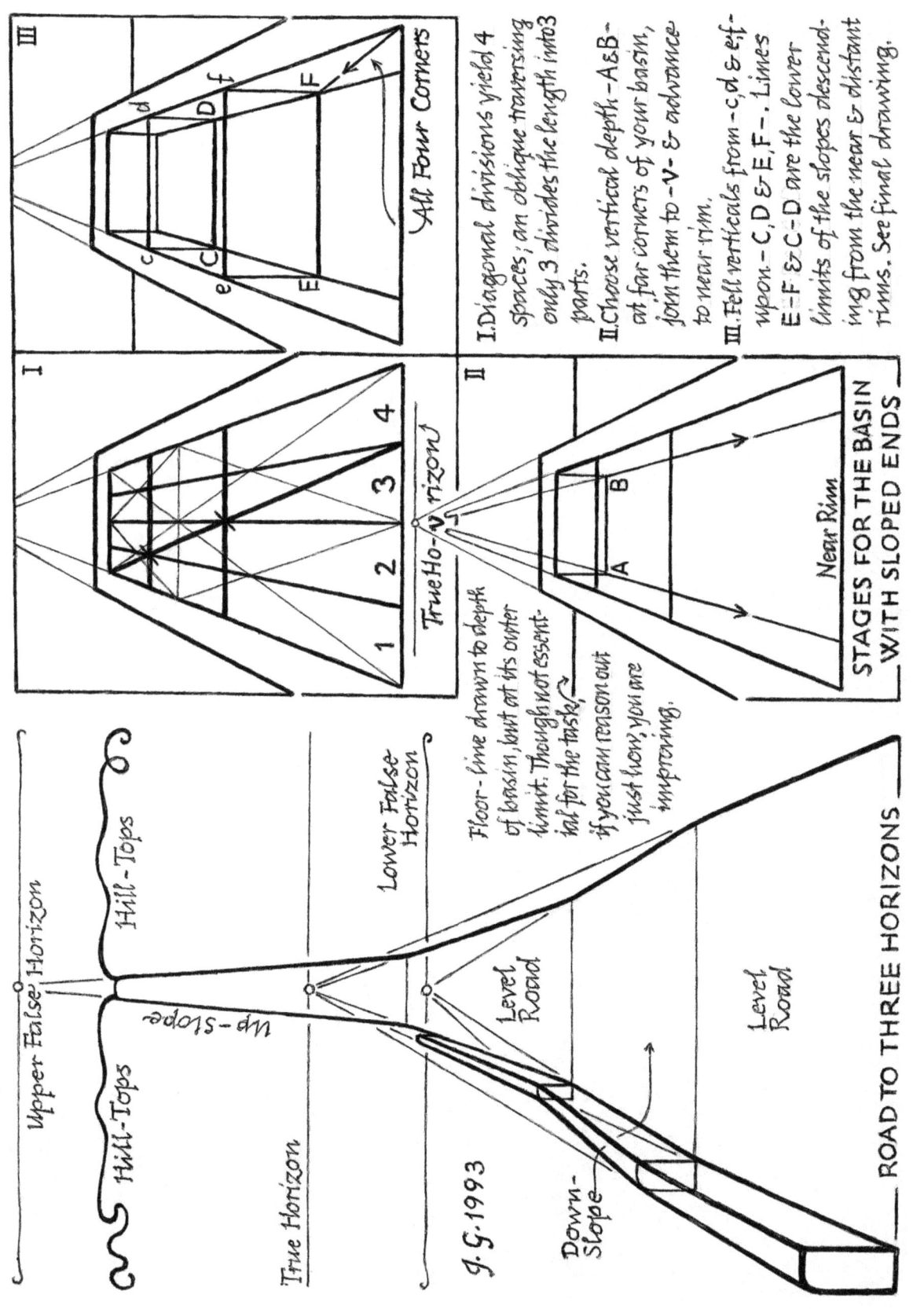

III    All Four Corners

I. Diagonal divisions yield 4 spaces; an oblique traversing only 3 divides the length into 3 parts.

II. Choose vertical depth – A & B – at far corners of your basin, join them to –v– & advance to near rim.

III. Fell verticals from –c,d & e,f– upon – C, D & E, F –. Lines E–F & C–D are the lower limits of the slopes descending from the near & distant rims. See final drawing.

I    True Ho– v rizon    1  2  3  4

II    A  B    Near Rim

STAGES FOR THE BASIN WITH SLOPED ENDS

Floor-line drawn to depth of basin, but at its outer limit. Though not essential for the task, if you can reason out just how, you are improving.

Upper False Horizon

Hill-Tops    Hill-Tops

True Horizon

Lower False Horizon

Up-slope

Level Road

Down-Slope

Level Road

g.g. 1993

ROAD TO THREE HORIZONS

**III.** Diagonal divisions yield the perspective horizontal mid-lines at the top & bottom. Verticals from *A* & *B* to their counterparts above cut the sides of every level at the corresponding points.

The horizontal lines between those points will be at the perspective midlines so the perspective midlines of the circles foreshortened to ellipses.

Erase no longer needed lines along the way.

---

**I.** Diagonal divisions into 4 spaces yield 5 horizontal levels & a vertical center line.

__C-entral V-anishing Point & Eye-Level__

Eye-level & C.V. are set, so that no level repeats another.

## STAGES FOR A 5 TIER CYLINDER

**II.** Vanishing lines join the ends of the 5 horizontals to V.C.

The depth of the base square is estimated & drawn as line A-B.

Verticals from A & B cut all vanishing lines at the contact for corners of each level.

Lines parallelling A-B join the corners & set the distant horizontal limits of each level.

---

**IV.** The apparent mid-line, cutting the ellipses into equal, level halves, extends beyond the true perspective line.

Verticals through the end-points of these apparent long diameters are the visible limits of the cylindric wall.

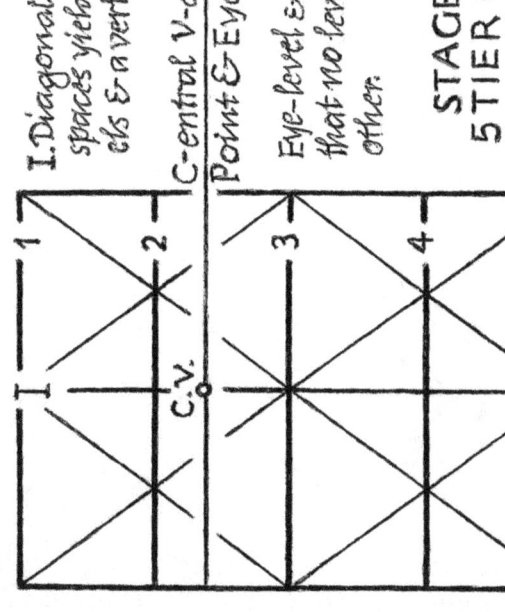

*Apparent Midline*

*True Perspective Mid-lines*

*Apparent Midline*

J.G. 1993

PLATE 19

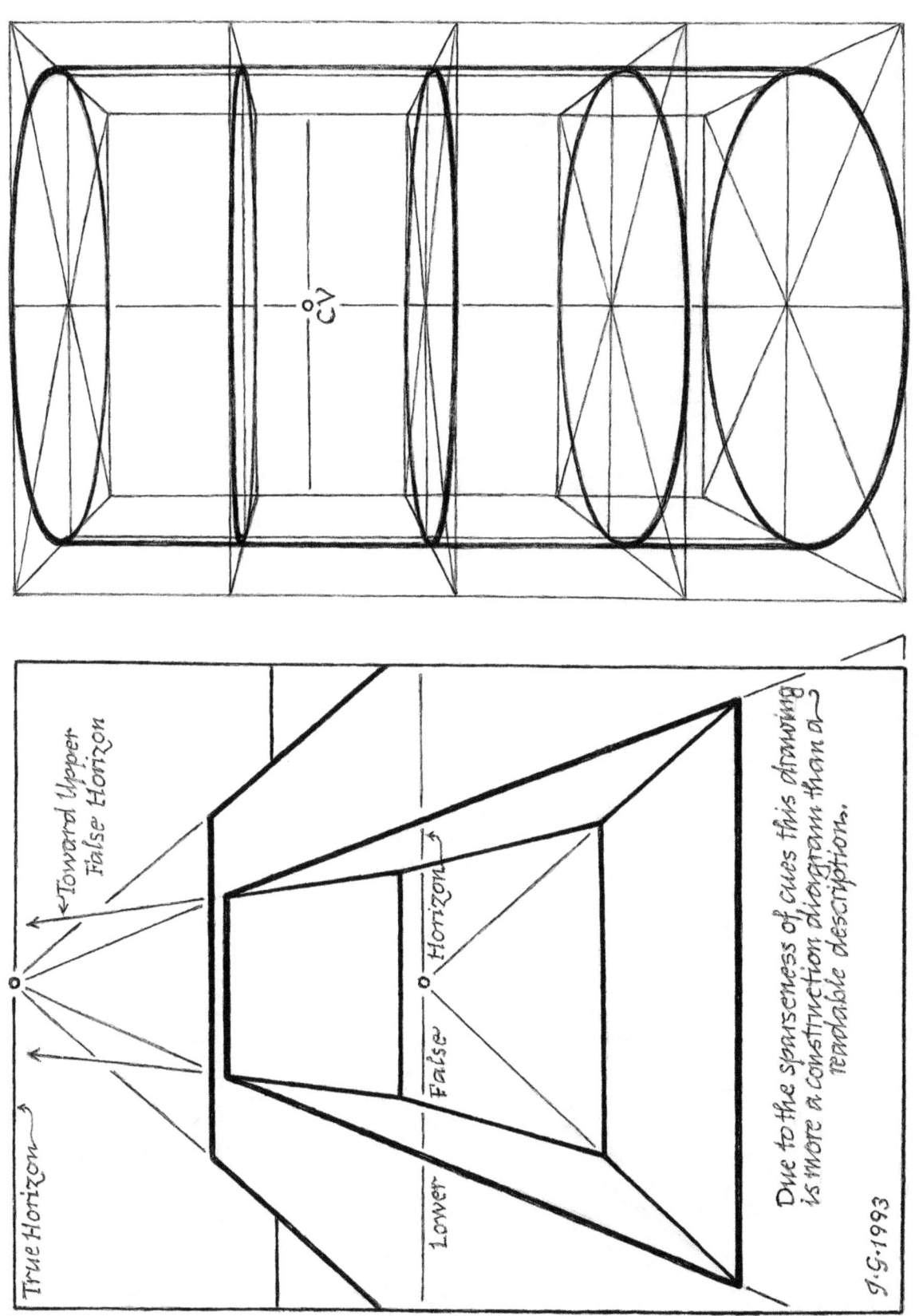

True Horizon →

←Toward Upper
False Horizon

← False Horizon

Lower False

Due to the sparseness of cues this drawing
is more a construction diagram than a
readable description.

J.G.1993

CV

PLATE 20

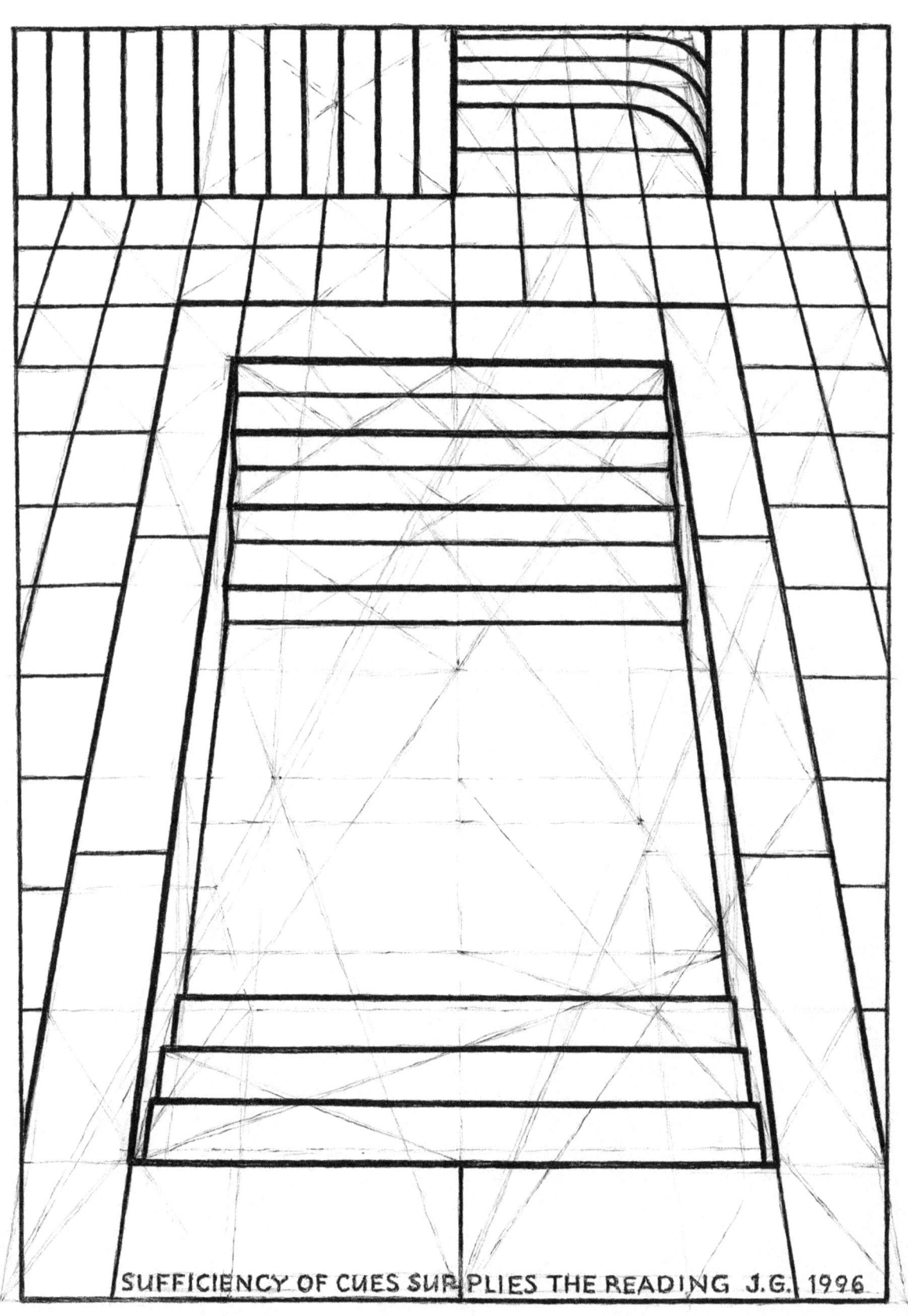

SUFFICIENCY OF CUES SUR PLIES THE READING   J.G. 1996

PLATE 21

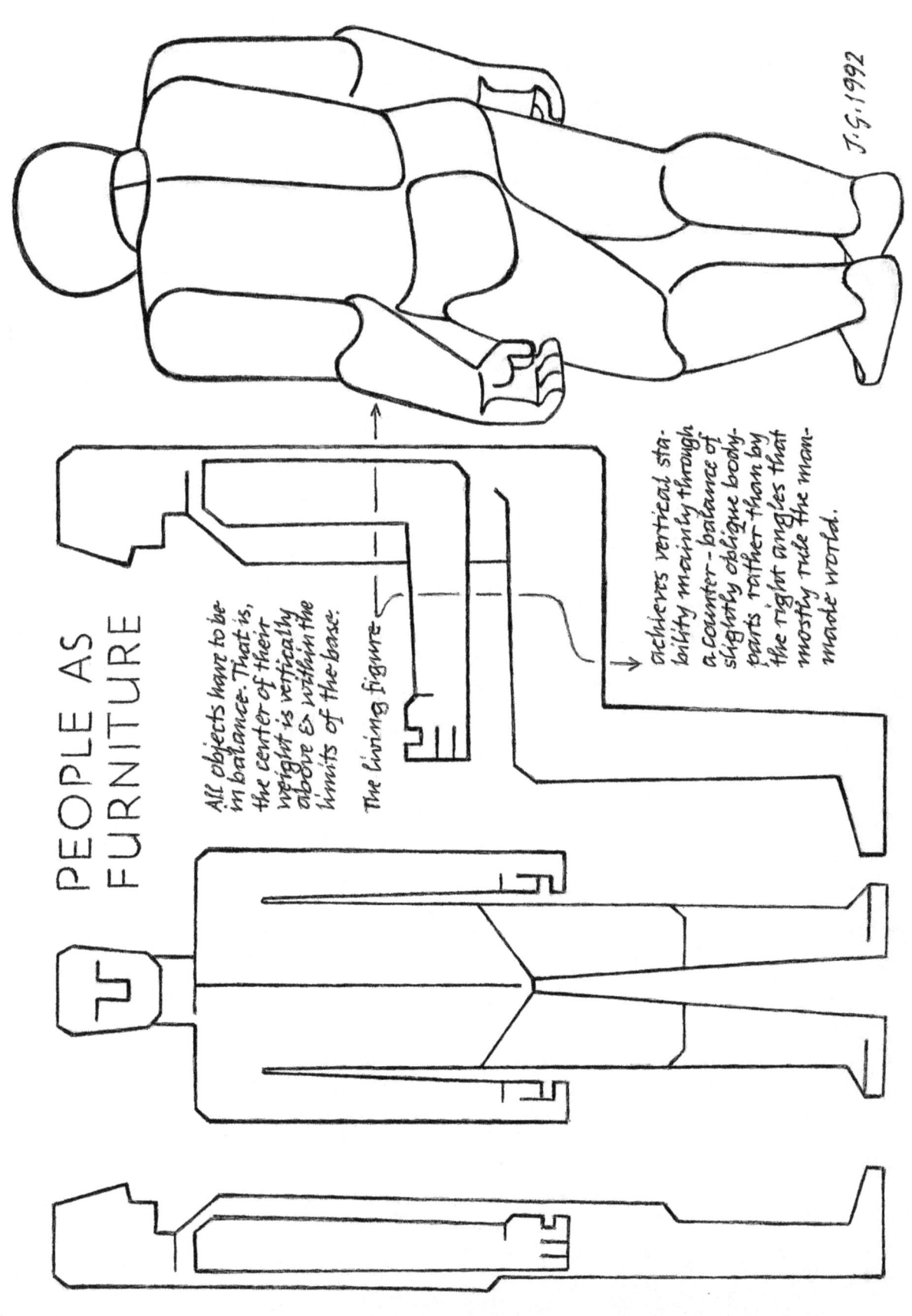

PEOPLE AS
FURNITURE

All objects have to be
in balance. That is,
the center of their
weight is vertically
above & within the
limits of the base.

The living figure

achieves vertical sta-
bility mainly through
a counter - balance of
slightly oblique body-
parts rather than by
the right angles that
mostly rule the man-
made world.

J.G. 1992

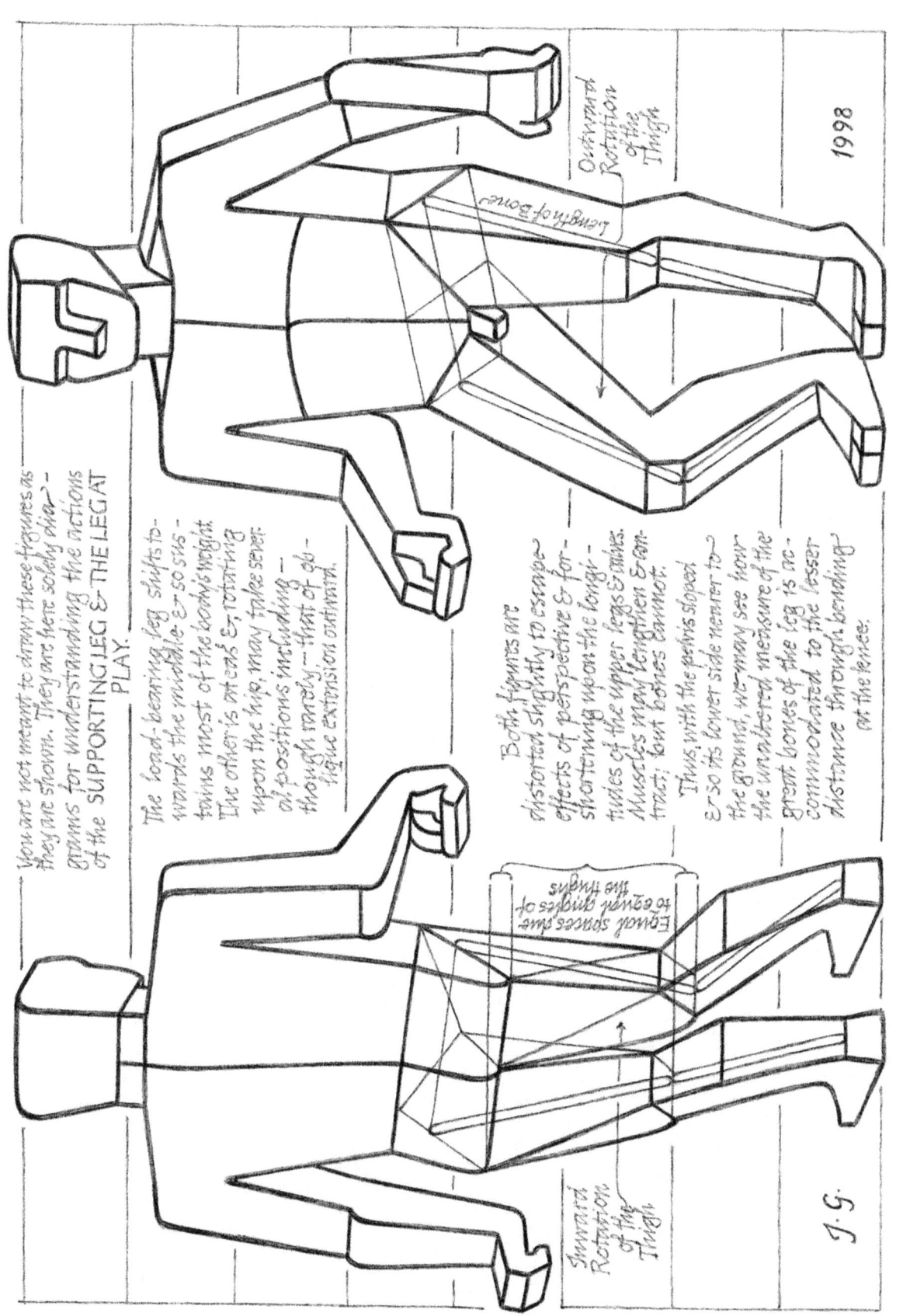

You are not meant to draw these figures as they are shown. They are here solely dia-grams for understanding the actions of the SUPPORTING LEG & THE LEG AT PLAY.

The load-bearing leg shifts to-wards the middle & so sus-tains most of the body's weight. The other is at ease, rotating upon the hip, & may take sever-al positions including — though rarely — that of ob-lique extension outward.

Both figures are distorted slightly to escape effects of perspective & for-shortening upon the longi-tudes of the upper legs & thighs. Muscles may lengthen & con-tract; but bones cannot.

Thus, with the pelvis sloped & so its lower side nearer to the ground, we may see how the unaltered measure of the great bones of the leg is ac-commodated to the lesser distance through bending at the knee.

Outward Rotation of the Thigh

Length of Bone

1998

Equal spaces due to equal angles of the thighs

Inward Rotation of the Thigh

J.G.

PLATE 23

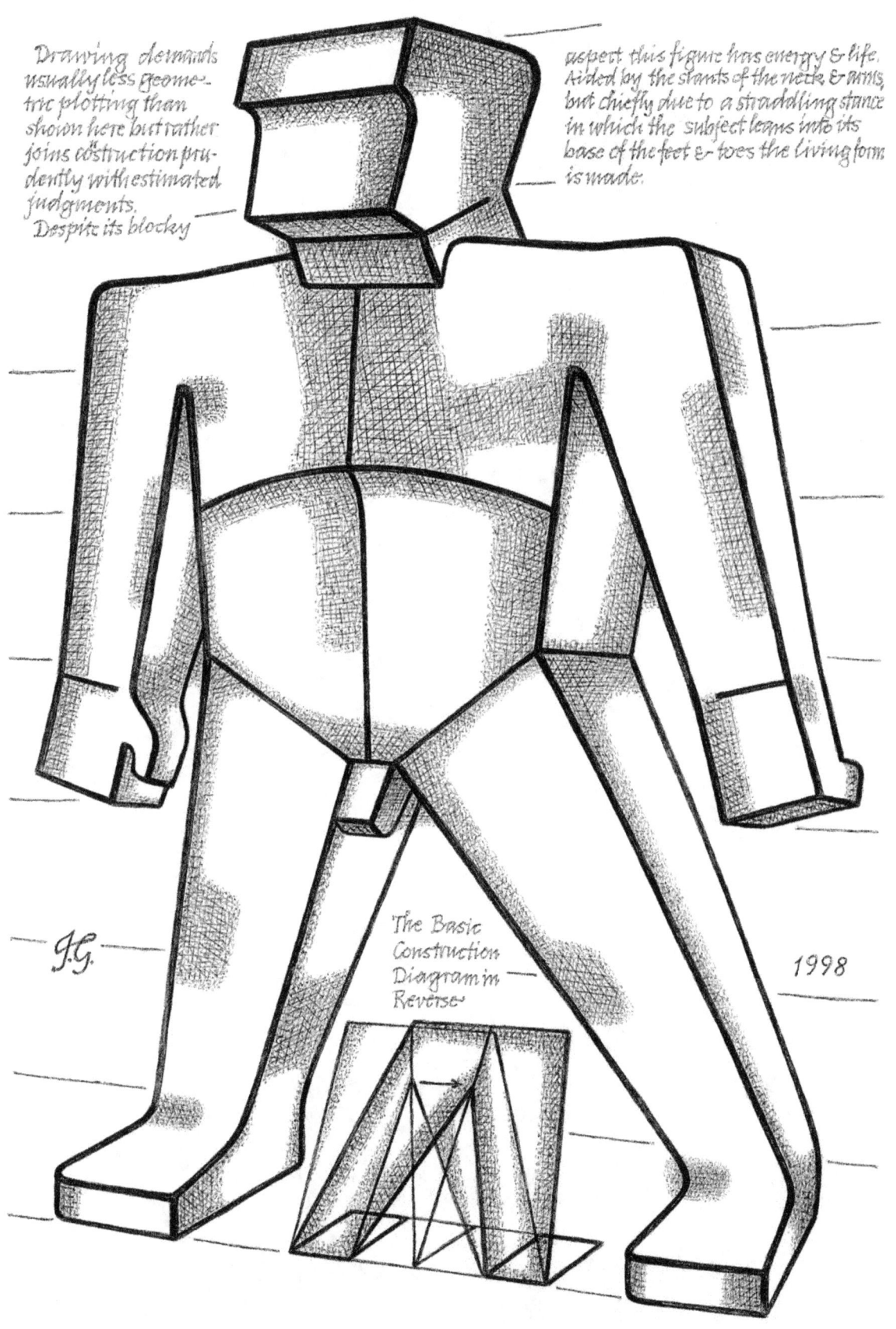

Drawing demands
usually less geome-
tric plotting than
shown here but rather
joins construction pru-
dently with estimated
judgments.
    Despite its blocky

aspect this figure has energy & life.
Aided by the slants of the neck & arms,
but chiefly due to a straddling stance
in which the subject leans into its
base of the feet & toes the living form
is made.

J.G.

The Basic
Construction
Diagram in
Reverse

1998

PLATE 24

THE BASIC
MASSING

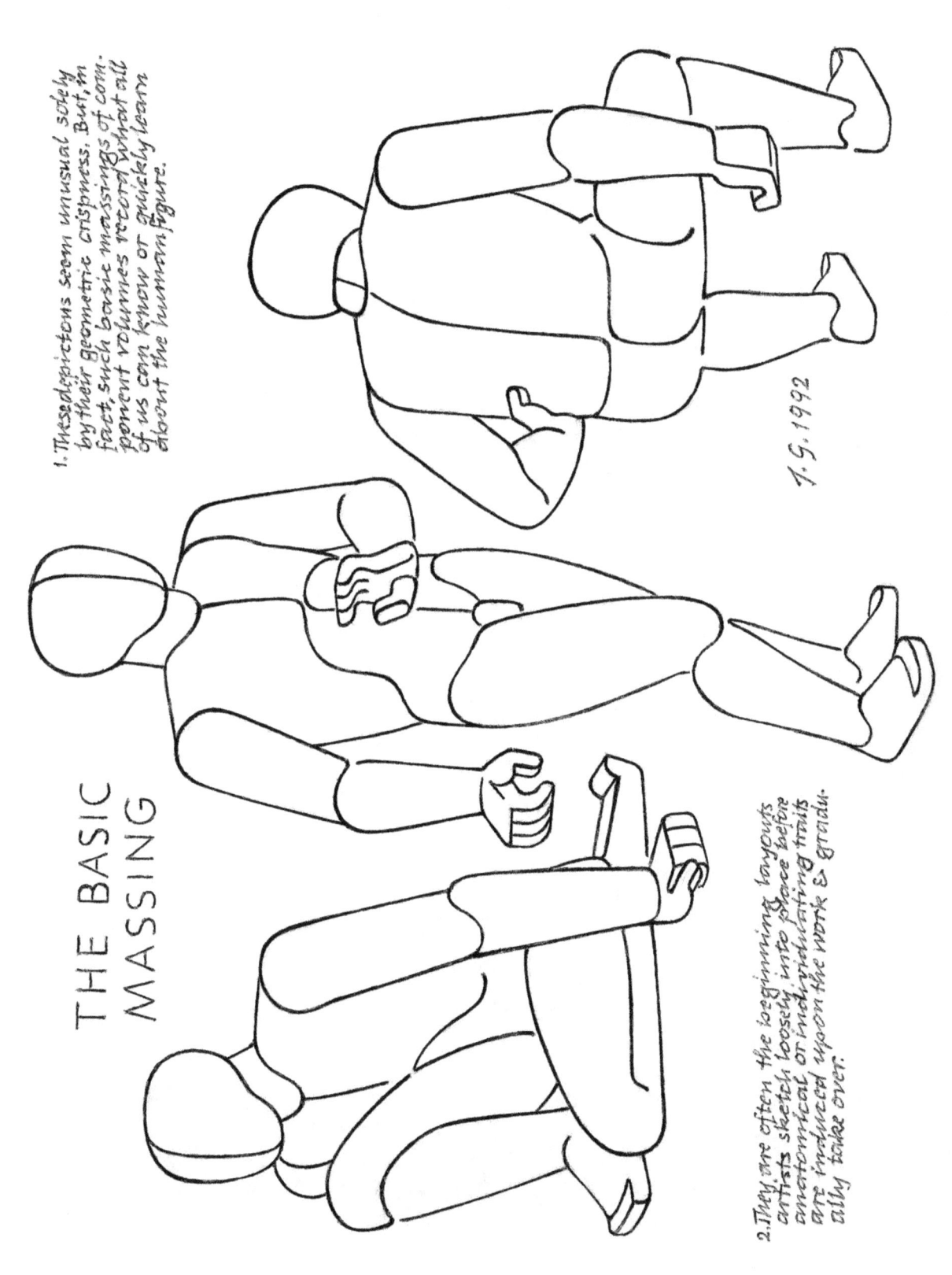

1. These depictions seem unusual solely by their geometric crispness. But, in fact, such basic massings of component volumes record what all of us can know or quickly learn about the human figure.

2. They are often the beginning layouts artists sketch loosely into place before anatomical or individuating traits are induced upon the work & gradually take over.

J.G. 1992

PLATE 25

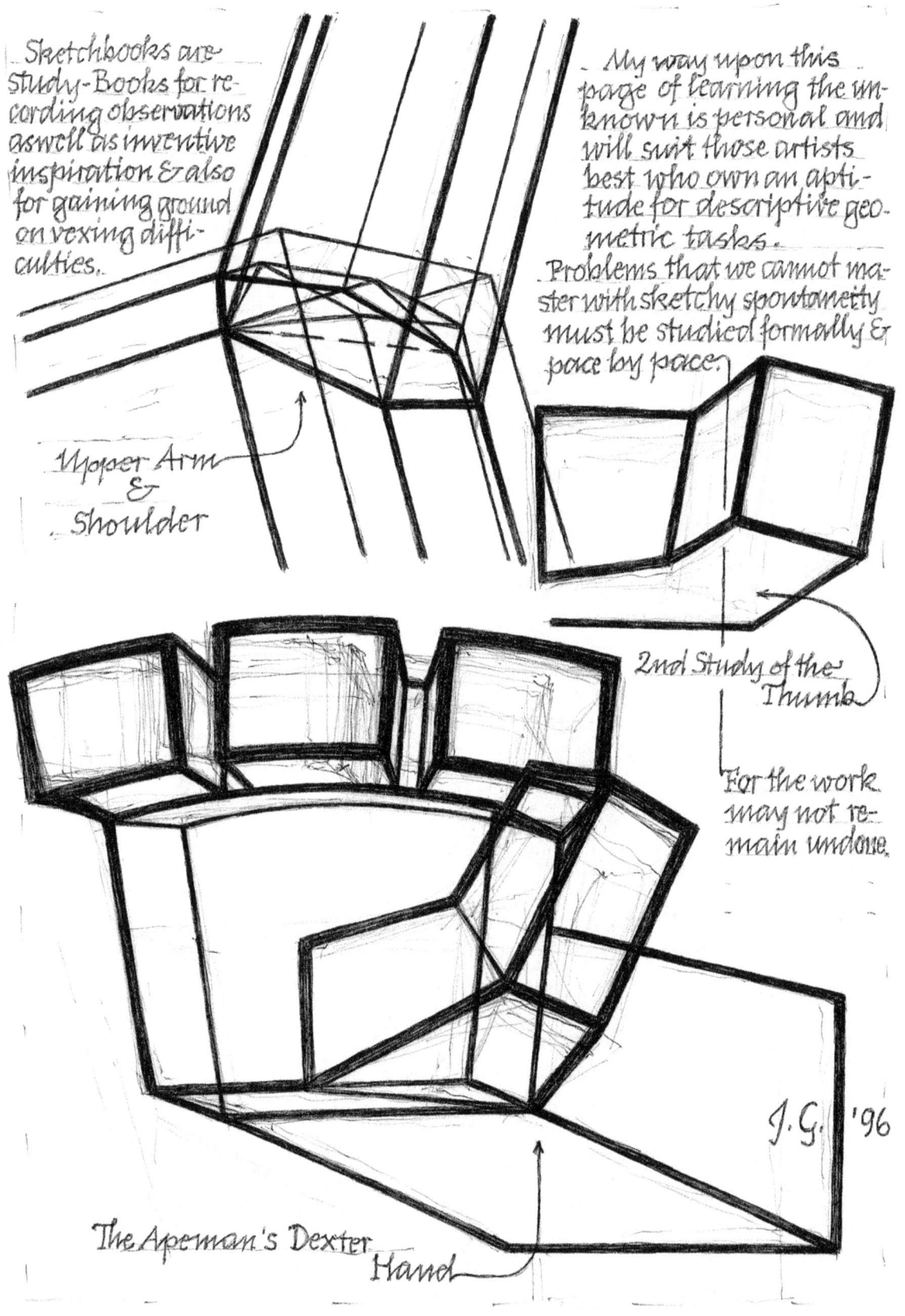

Sketchbooks are
study-Books for re-
cording observations
as well as inventive
inspiration & also
for gaining ground
on vexing diffi-
culties.

. My way upon this
page of learning the un-
known is personal and
will suit those artists
best who own an apti-
tude for descriptive geo-
metric tasks.
Problems that we cannot master with sketchy spontaneity
must be studied formally &
pace by pace.

Upper Arm
&
Shoulder

2nd Study of the
Thumb

For the work
may not re-
main undone.

J.G. '96

The Apeman's Dexter
Hand

PLATE 26

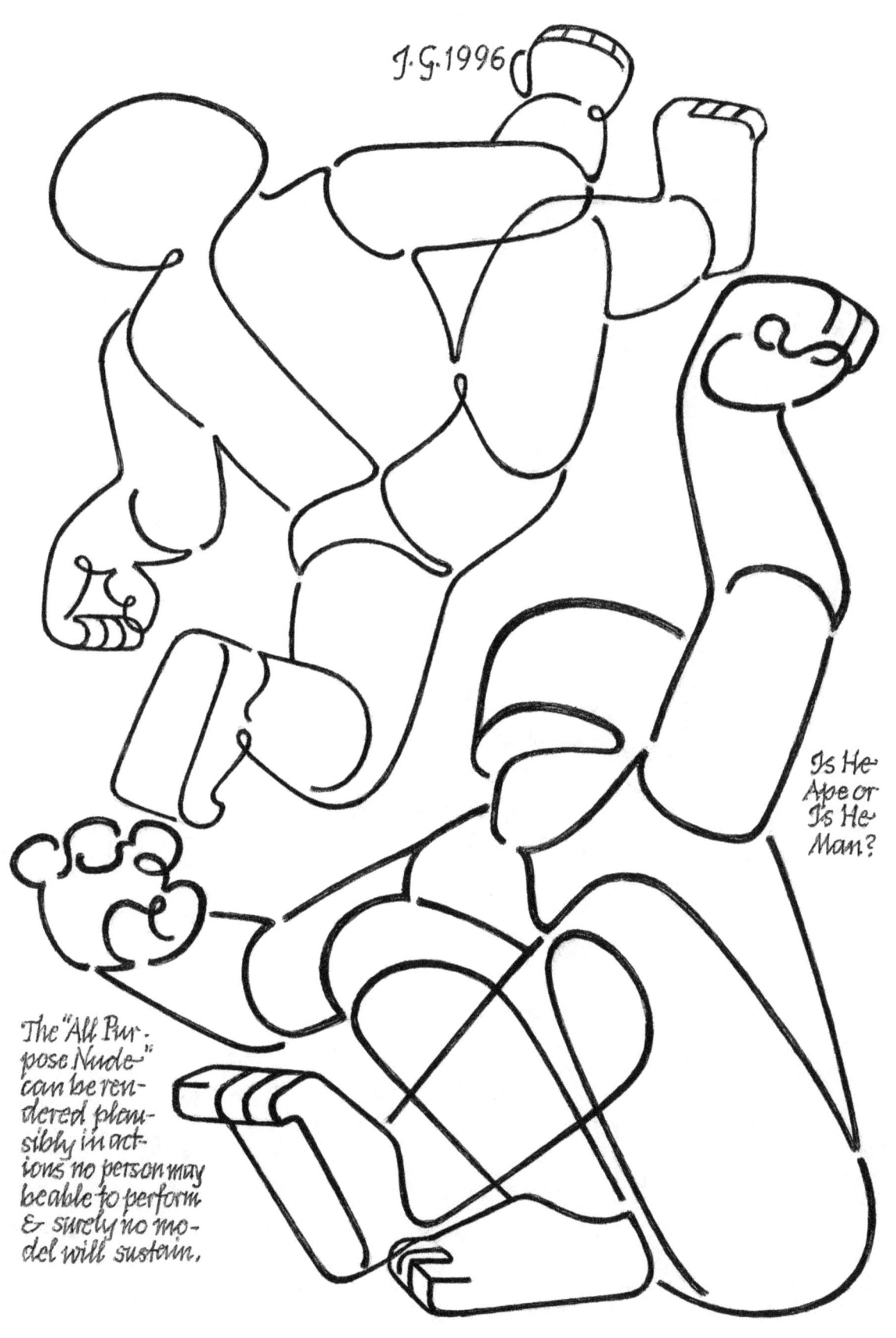

J.G.1996

Is He
Ape or
Is He
Man?

The "All Pur-
pose Nude"
can be ren-
dered plau-
sibly in act-
ions no person may
be able to perform
& surely no mo-
del will sustain.

PLATE 27

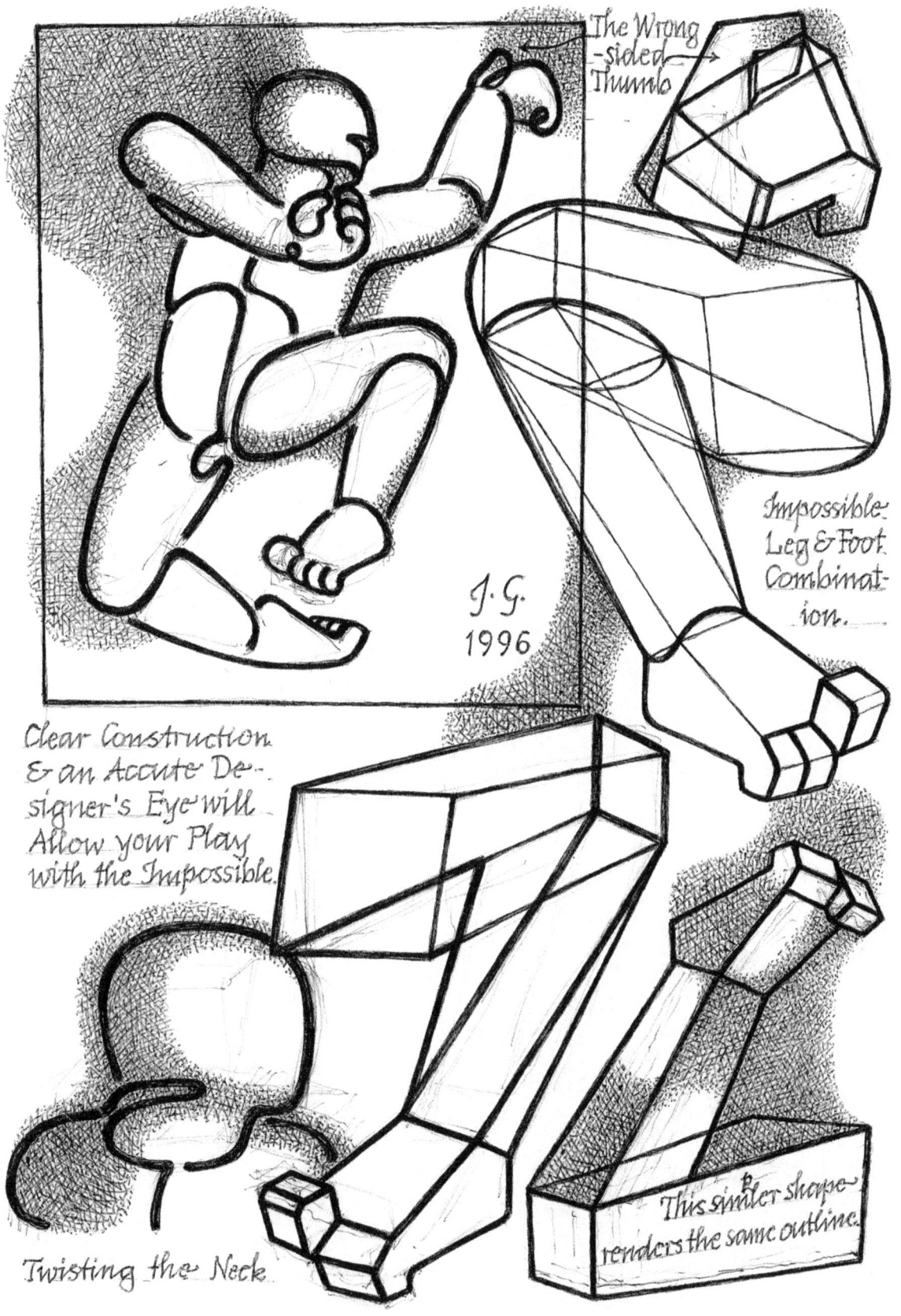

The Wrong
-sided
Thumb

Impossible
Leg & Foot
Combinat-
ion.

Clear Construction
& an Accute De-
signer's Eye will
Allow your Play
with the Impossible.

J. G.
1996

Twisting the Neck

This similar shape
renders the same outline.

PLATE 28

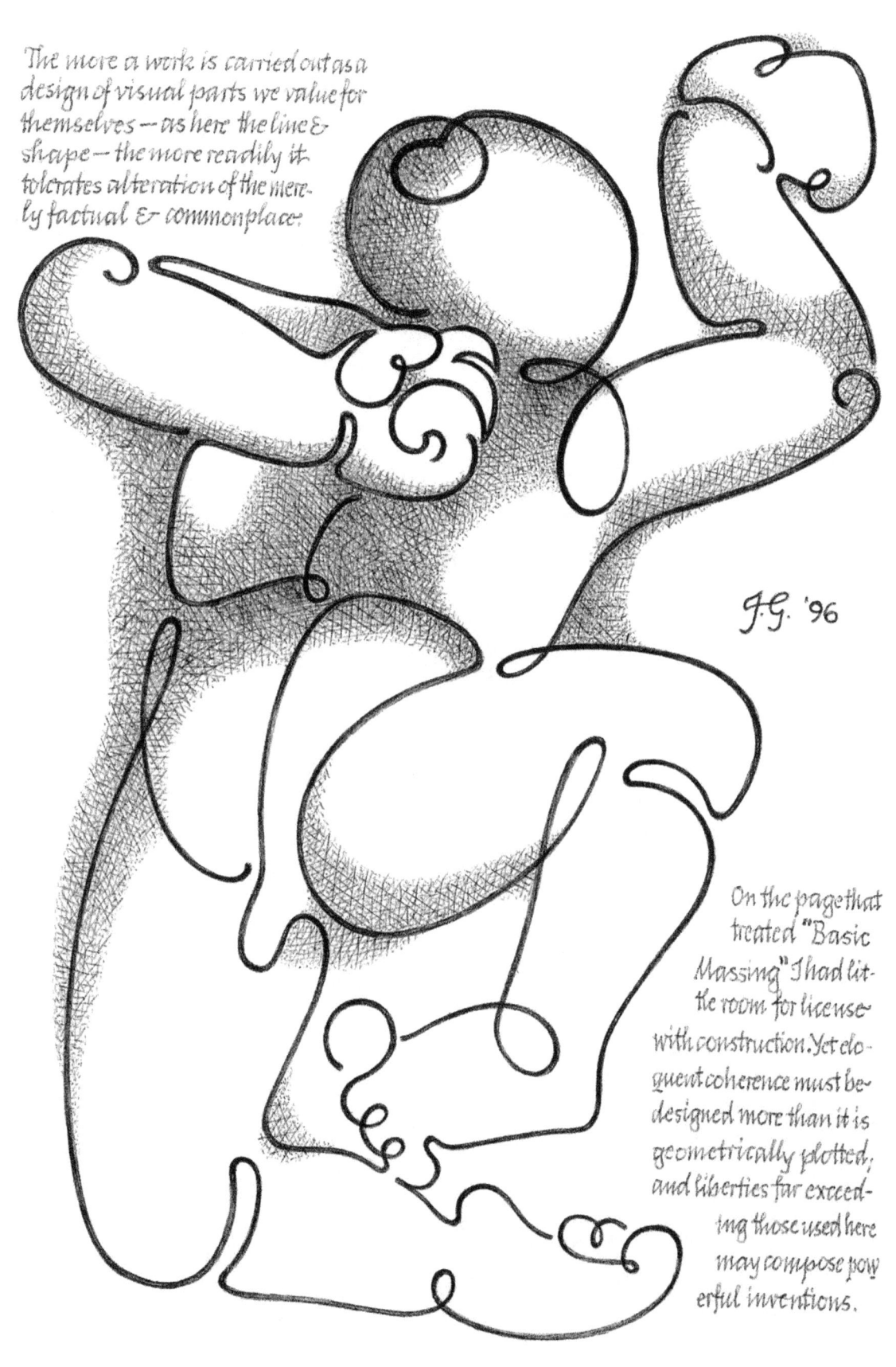

The more a work is carried out as a design of visual parts we value for themselves — as here the line & shape — the more readily it tolerates alteration of the merely factual & commonplace:

J·G· '96

On the page that treated "Basic Massing" I had little room for license with construction. Yet eloquent coherence must be designed more than it is geometrically plotted; and liberties far exceeding those used here may compose powerful inventions.

*PLATE 29*

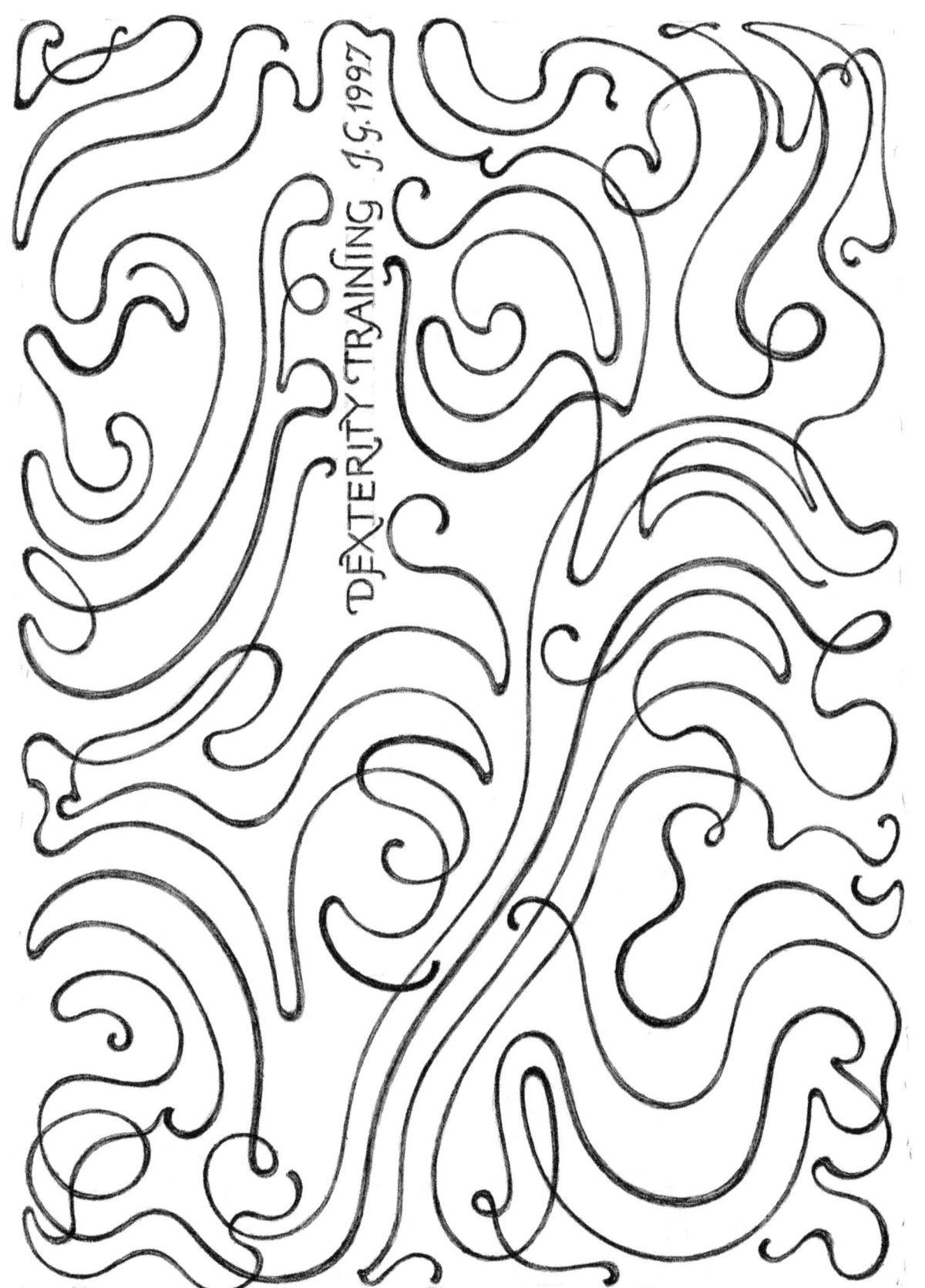

DEXTERITY TRAINING  1.9.1997

PLATE 30

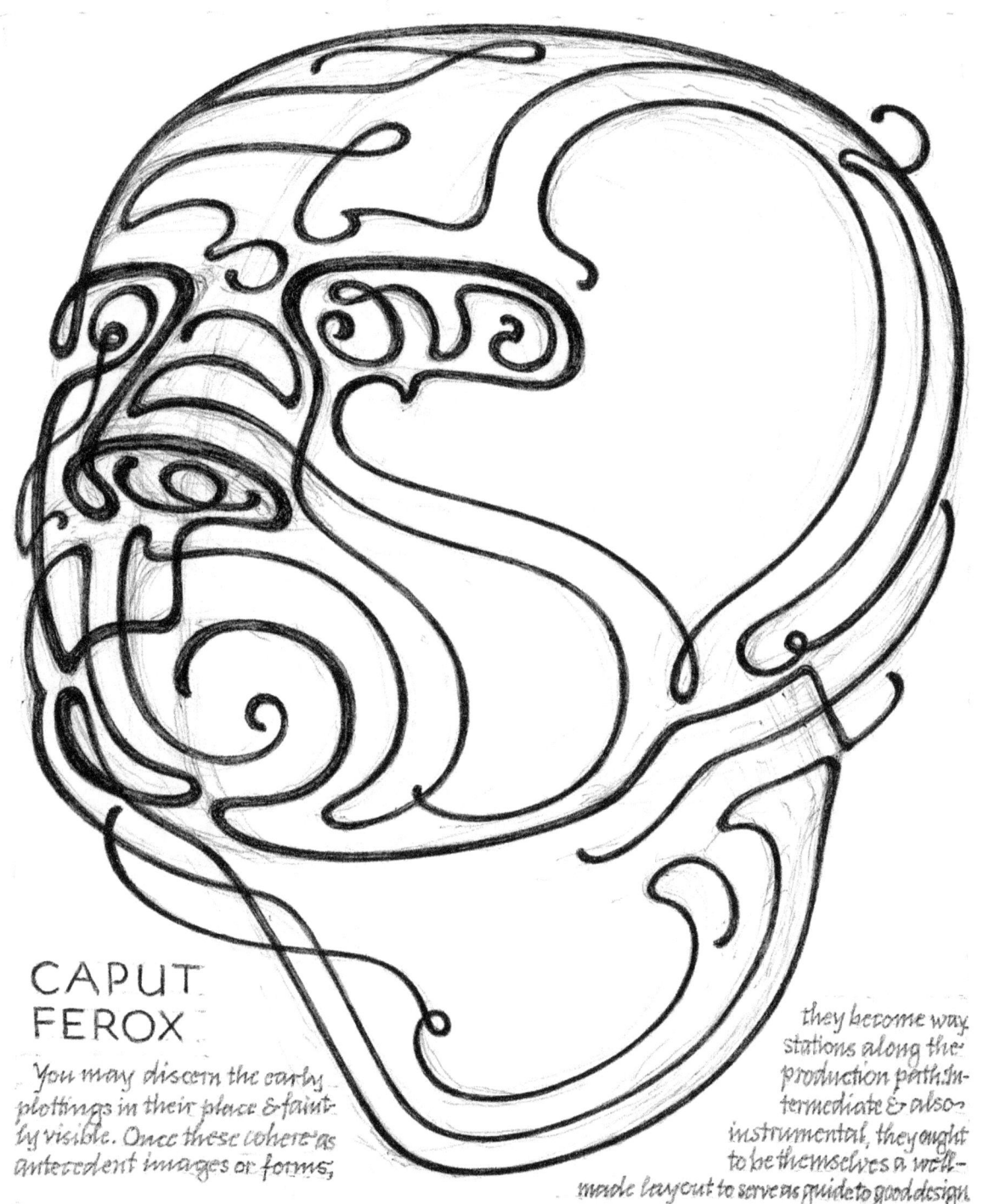

## CAPUT
## FEROX

You may discern the early
plottings in their place & faint-
ly visible. Once these cohere as
antecedent images or forms,

they become way
stations along the
production path. In-
termediate & also
instrumental, they ought
to be themselves a well-
made layout to serve as guide to good design.

The overlapping strokes, mainly
where the head & neck are joined, work like tone reducing contrasts at a boundary.
Some of the outline of a form may thus retreat, so that other parts — as here the fore-
head, nose & chin — will be able to advance.

J.G. 1997

*PLATE 31*

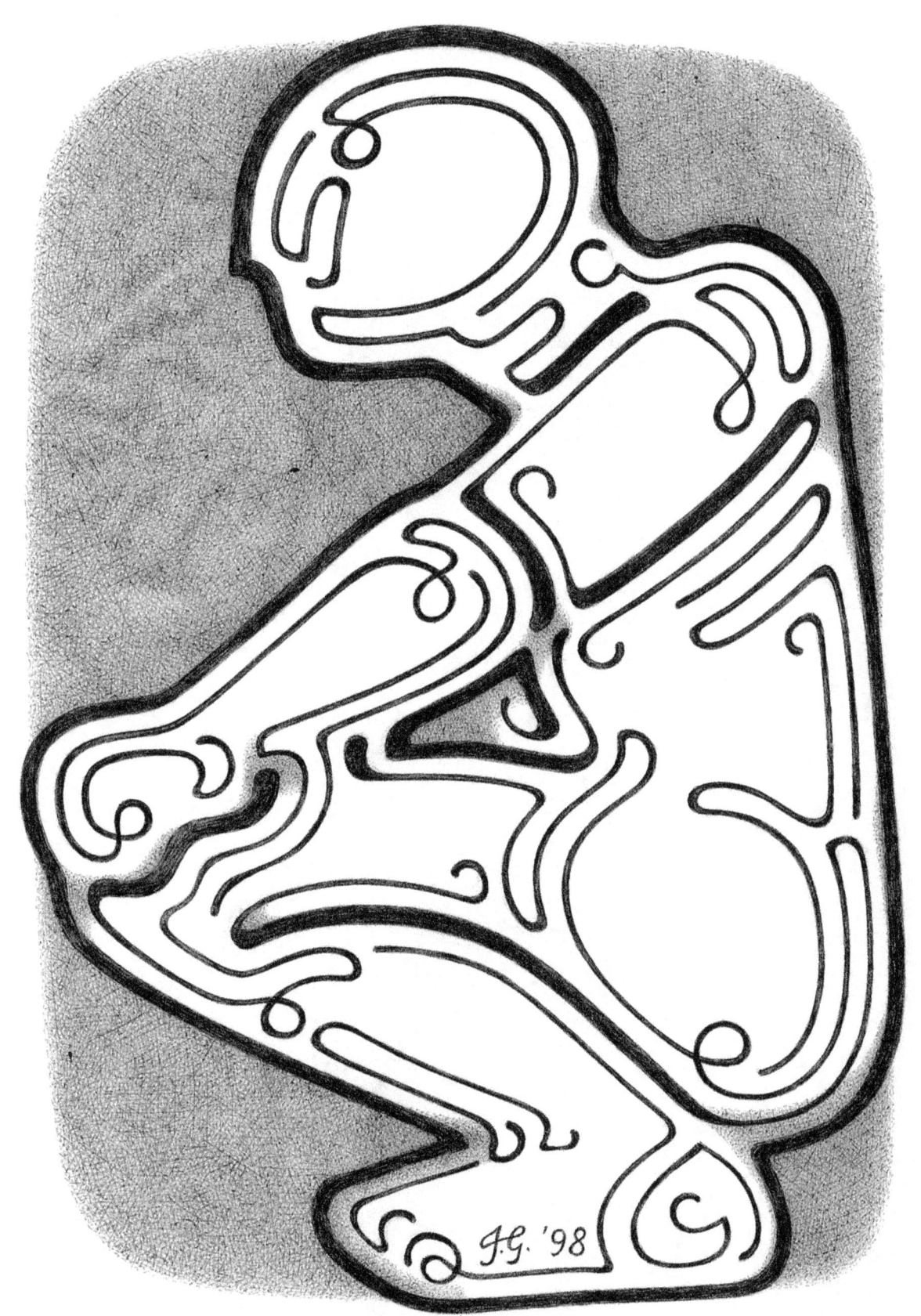

PLATE 32

# A LIBRARY of FORMS

A volume in heavy black & white has a different—more immediate—appeal, because it is more quickly seen, from one surrounded by an ambience of tone with its sense of light & atmosphere & even hint of color.

A solid rendered as a scientific geometrical projection may own a visual attraction but speaks eloquently most of all to our understanding, while this cylinder invites the viewer—stroke by stroke, to assemble my construct for himself.

Yet their descriptive clarity, in every case, is owed to the same cause—the elements composing them are always geometric parts of the volume whole.

In addition, it will help us to put these elements in place, so that clear lights & darks will contrast the adjacent planes along the identifying edges bounding the faces of the pyramid & cube as well as the wall & upper circle of the cylinder.

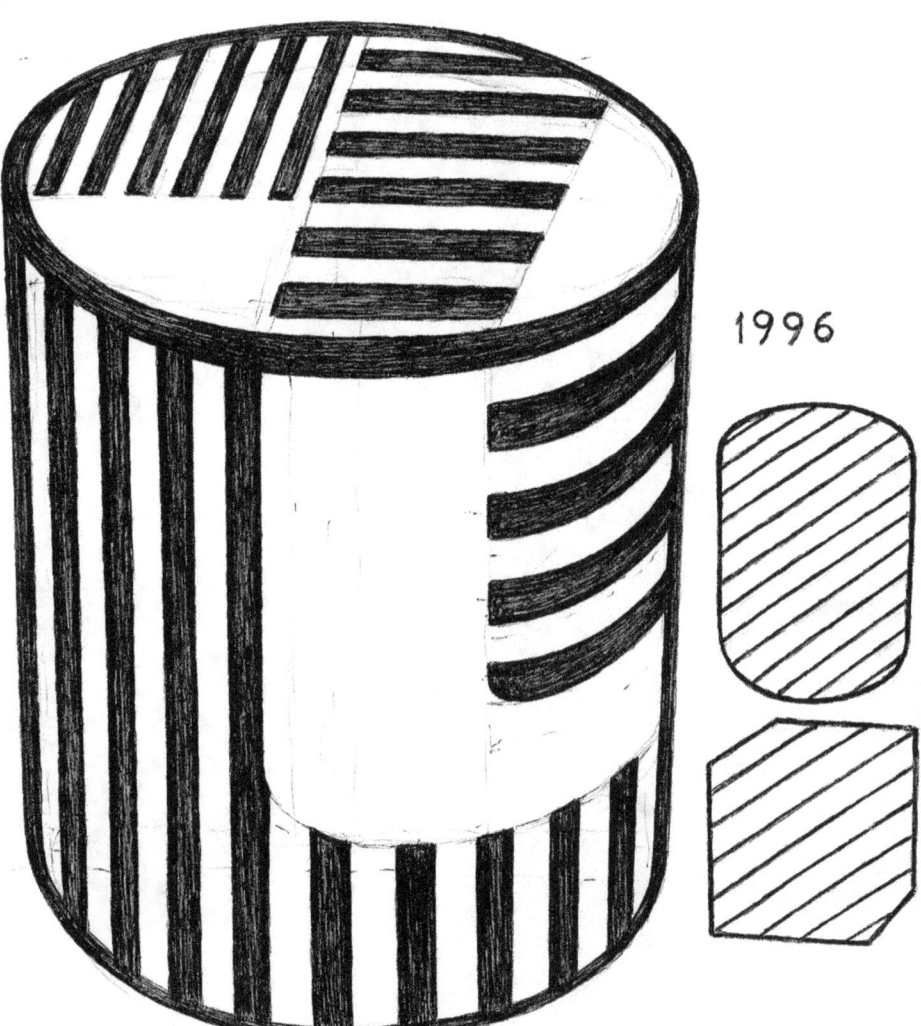

J.G.

1996

The contrast at the volume-building edges is really most important, as without them the cylinder & cube would only be such planar shapes as those shown on the right.

PLATE 33

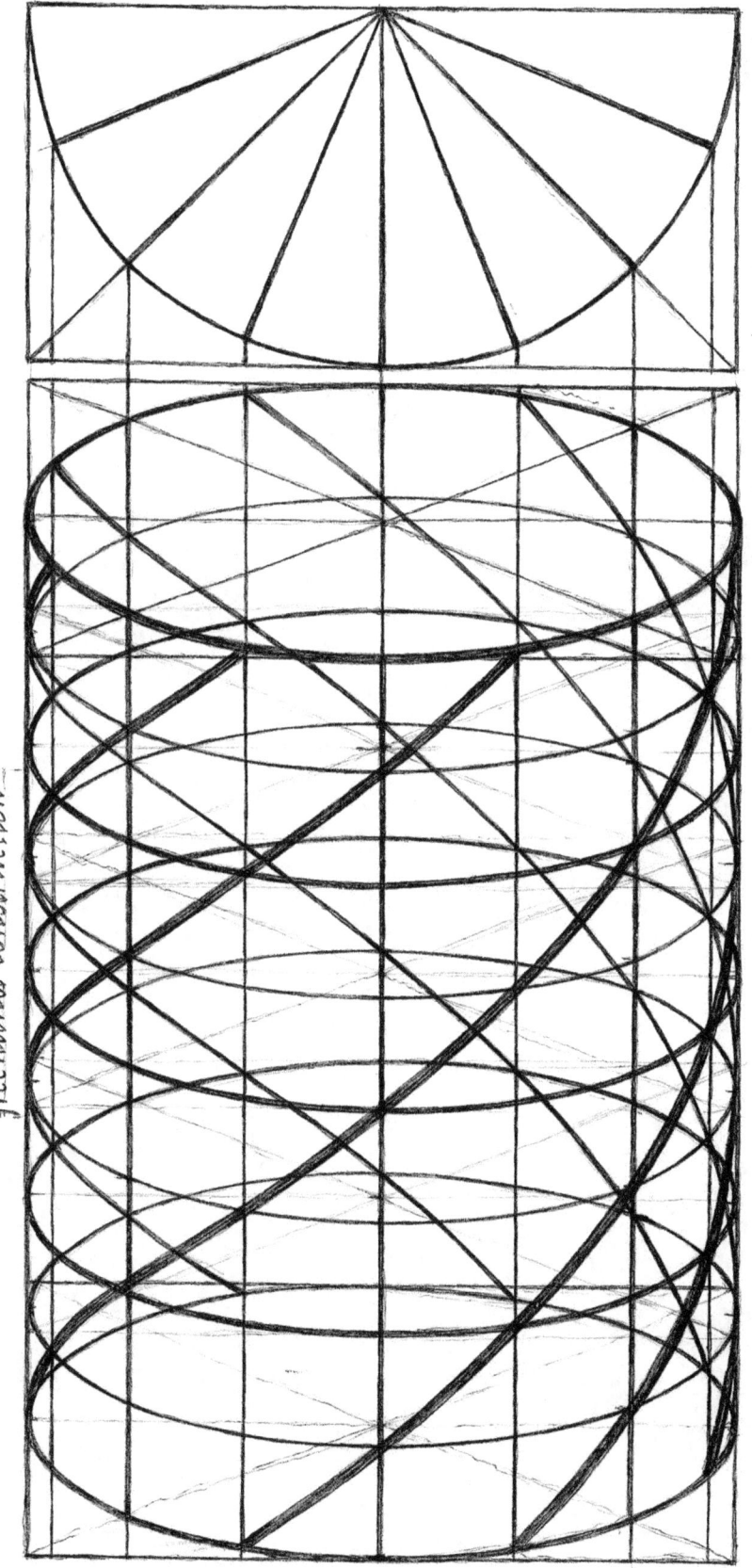

freehand construction...

PLATE 34

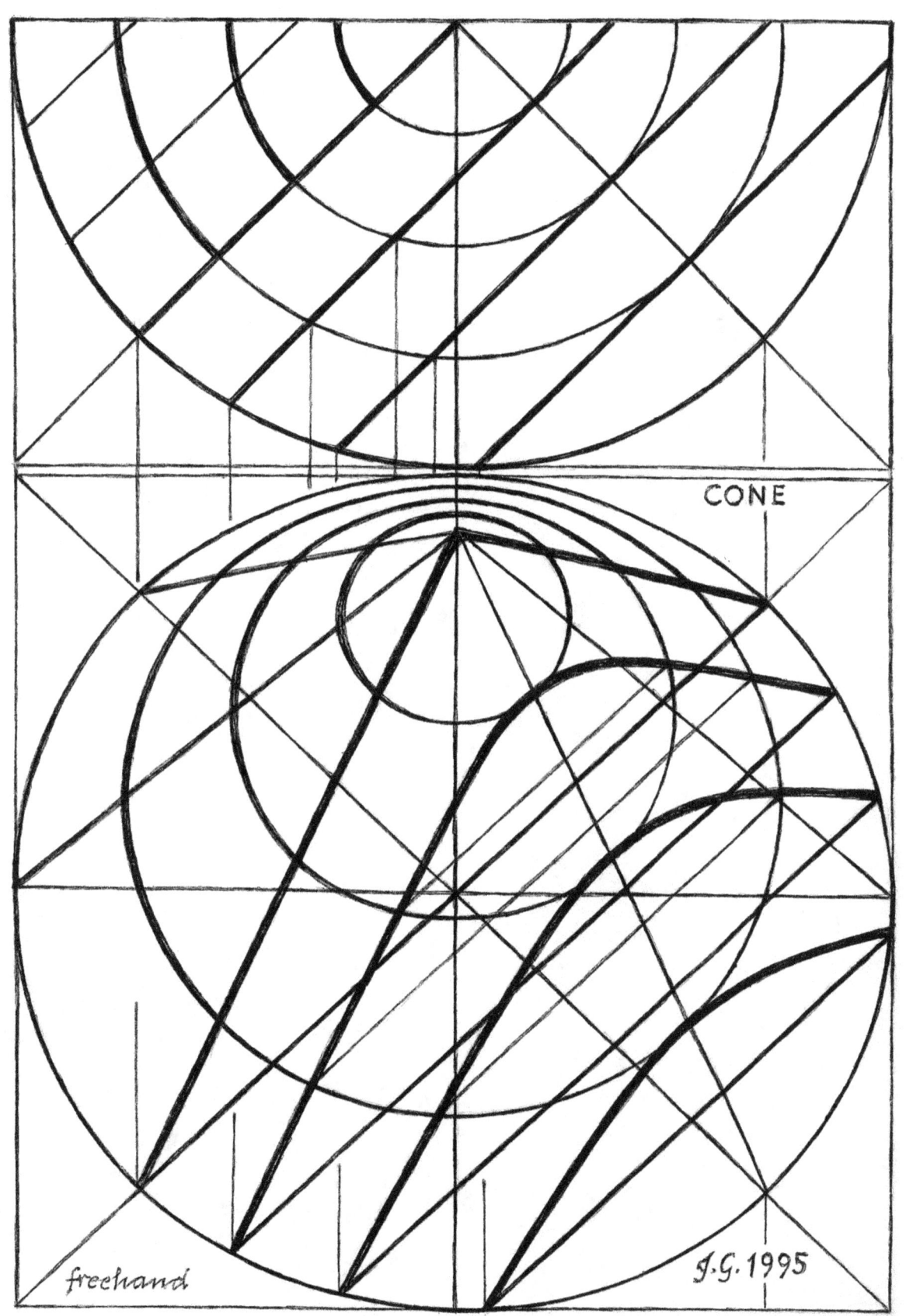

CONE

freehand

J.G. 1995

PLATE 35

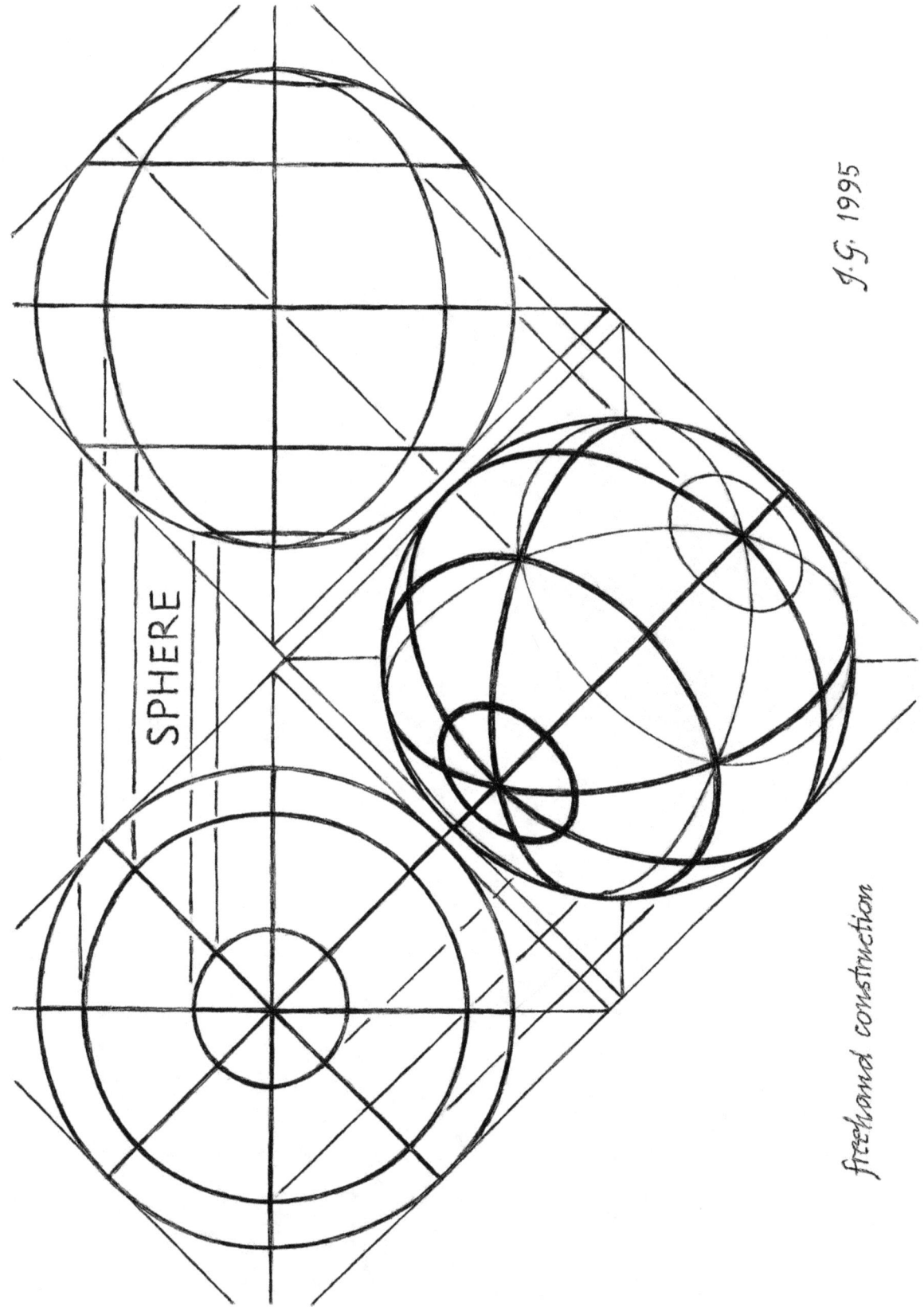

SPHERE

J.G. 1995

freehand construction

PLATE 36

## Points To Keep In Mind

1. The square base of a pyramid shortens in perspective & will show a bit more width than height.

2. A pyramidal peak rises above the crosspoint of the diagonals, while a pit is lowered beneath them.

3. The pit may best be shown through emphasis upon the solid rim rather than the sunken point.

4. Especially along the forward edges of the peak tones should grow in contrast as they close upon the point.

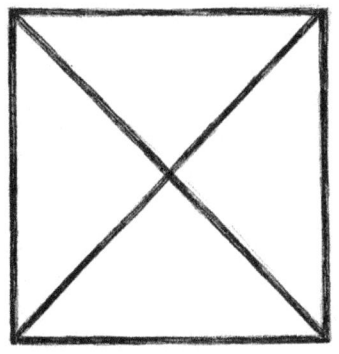

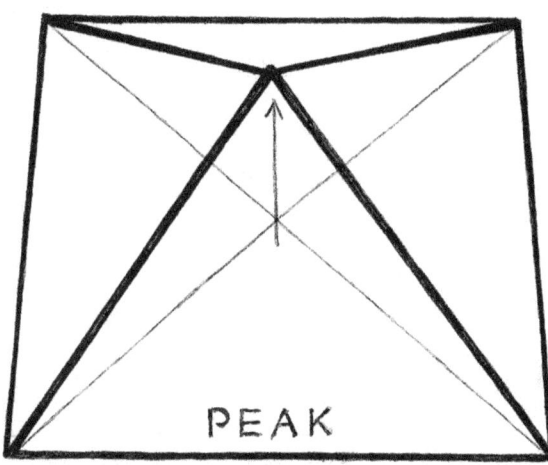

PEAK

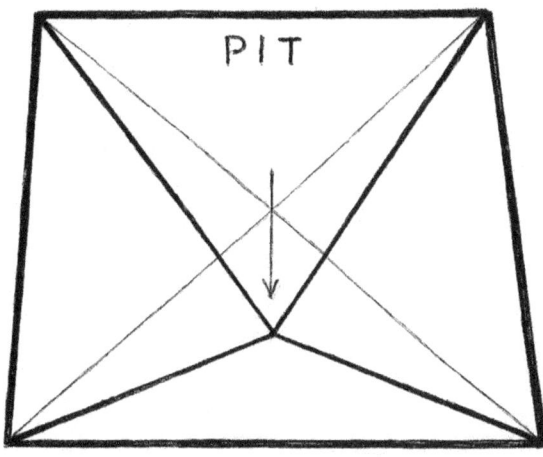

PIT

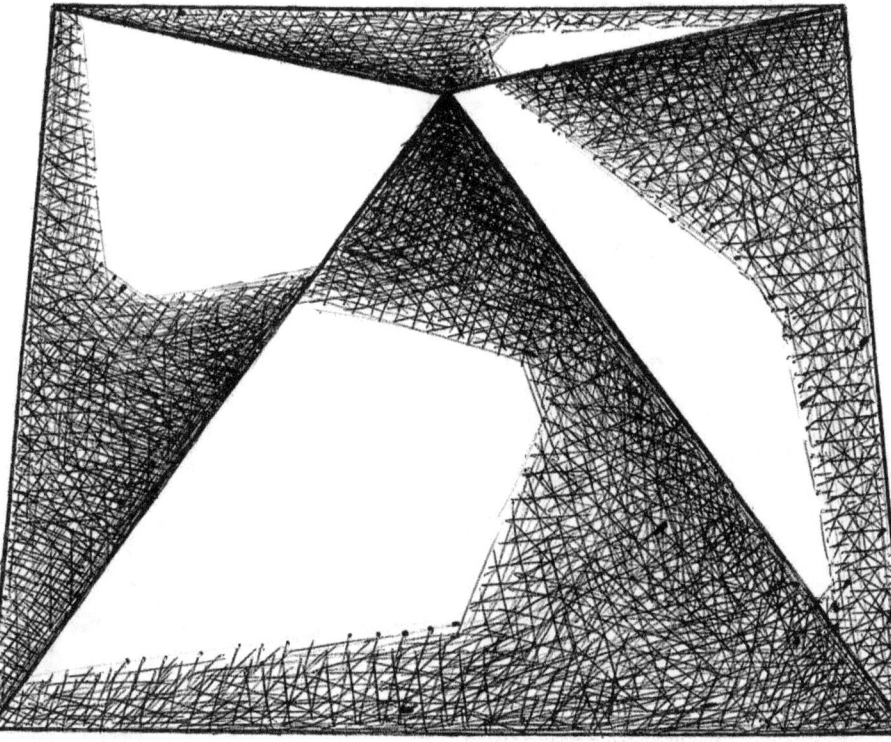

5. An adjustable tonal layout is begun, darkened as needed & its shapes made gradually firm.

6. Understand the demonstration,— do not imitate.

J. G.
1992

PLATE 37

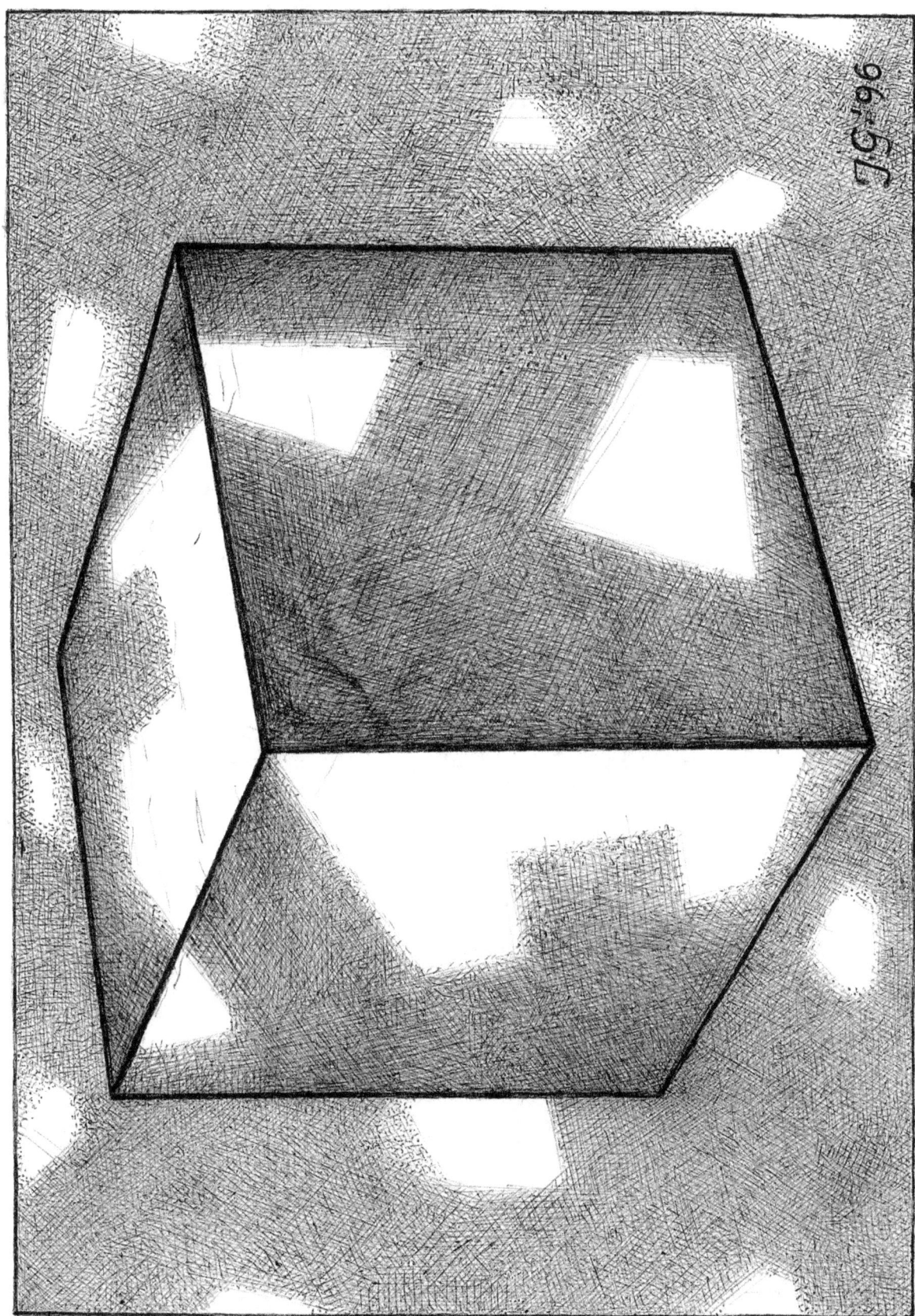

PLATE 38

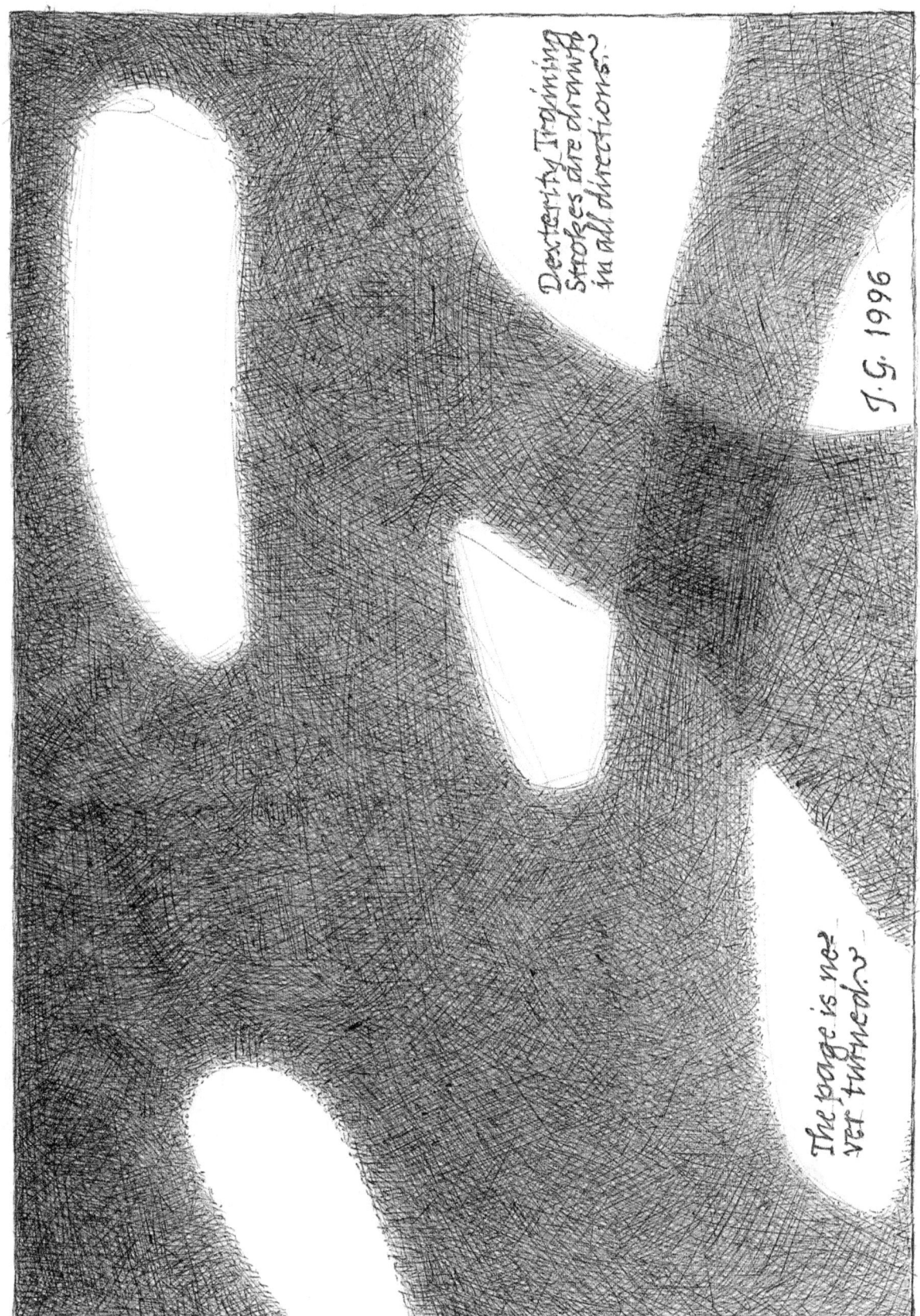

Dexterity Training
Strokes are drawn
in all directions~

J.S. 1996

The page is not
yet turned~

*PLATE 39*

Of the basic solids, this top view of the cone may be the hardest to articulate when light & shade are not employed to render the description.

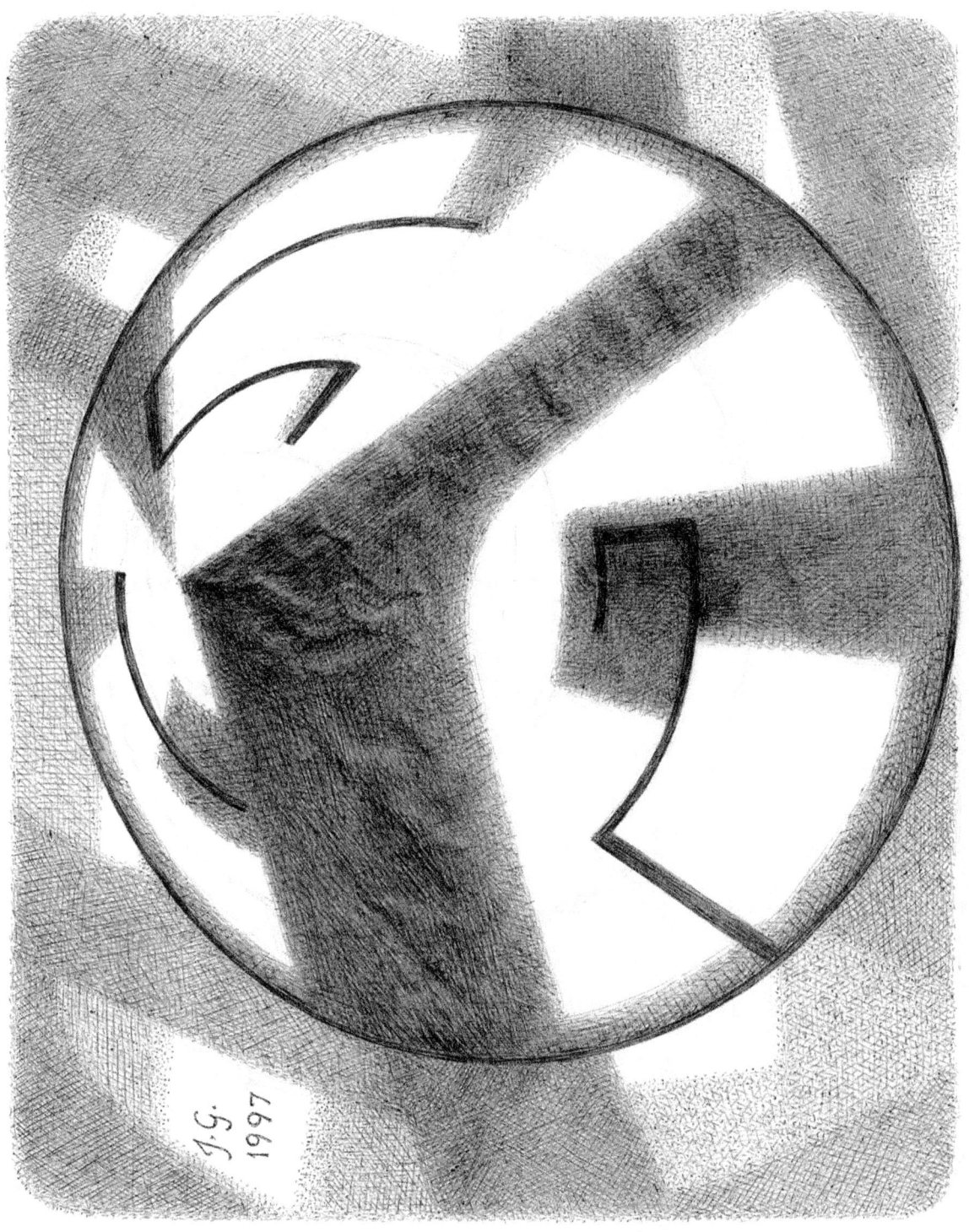

J.G.
1997

Besides the line & tone, blank spaces are also geometric sections of the whole and join the others in delivering the reading.

*PLATE 40*

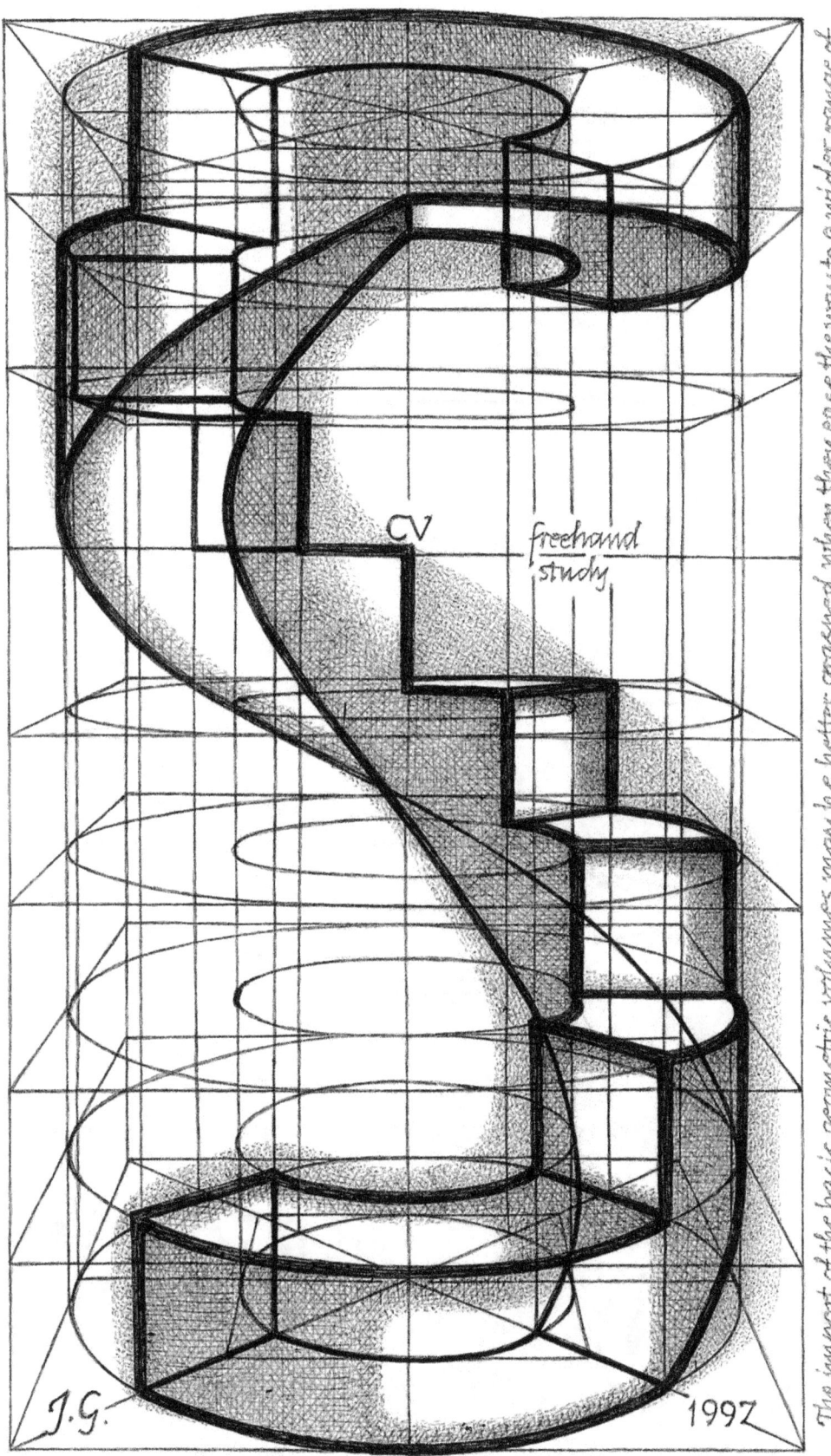

CV

freehand
study

J.G.

1992

The import of the basic geometric volumes may be better grasped when they ease the way to a wider range of subjects. Thus a plain right-angular solid could be transformed to yield the twisted shape in front; and know-ing how spiral turns traverse the walls of cylinders could gain this set of steps.

Full understanding of these simple volumes is not given to the artist. For this would mean the power to construct their every variant & elaboration and may well elude even the most able mathematician. We likely therefore have to end each line of study at the point of surplus learning just beyond the needs of our visual work.

*PLATE 41*

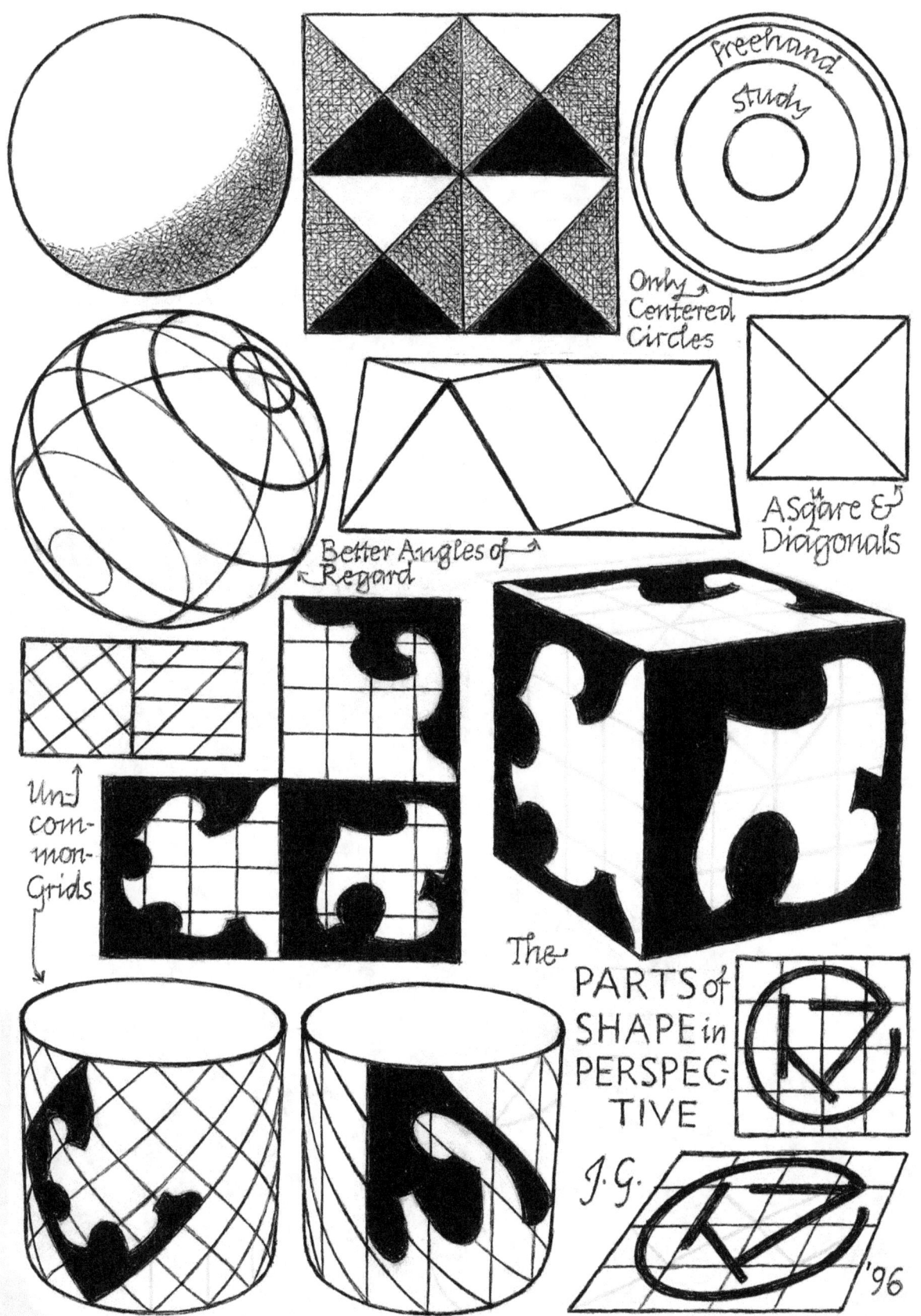

freehand study

Only Centered Circles

Better Angles of Regard

A Square & Diagonals

Un-com-mon-Grids

The PARTS of SHAPE in PERSPECTIVE

J.G.

'96

PLATE 42

The latitudes & meridians of the globe render here the grid design.

freehand
study

J.G.
1996

The LAW of FORM ARTICULATION is not a rule of light & shade, but of the geometrical accord of each part with the volume whole and serves us as a guide for treating all objects at once massive & detailed. this thus ubiquitous & universal as well as easy to grasp. For even shape arrays of great complexity can only parallel, slant or curve against the grid divisions of a surface.

Thus to realize the visual shifting of the parts of shape—the curve, oblique & elements parallel to the grid design—within the perspective of a solid, is to own a potent tool for describing all forms in all possible ways.

PLATE 43

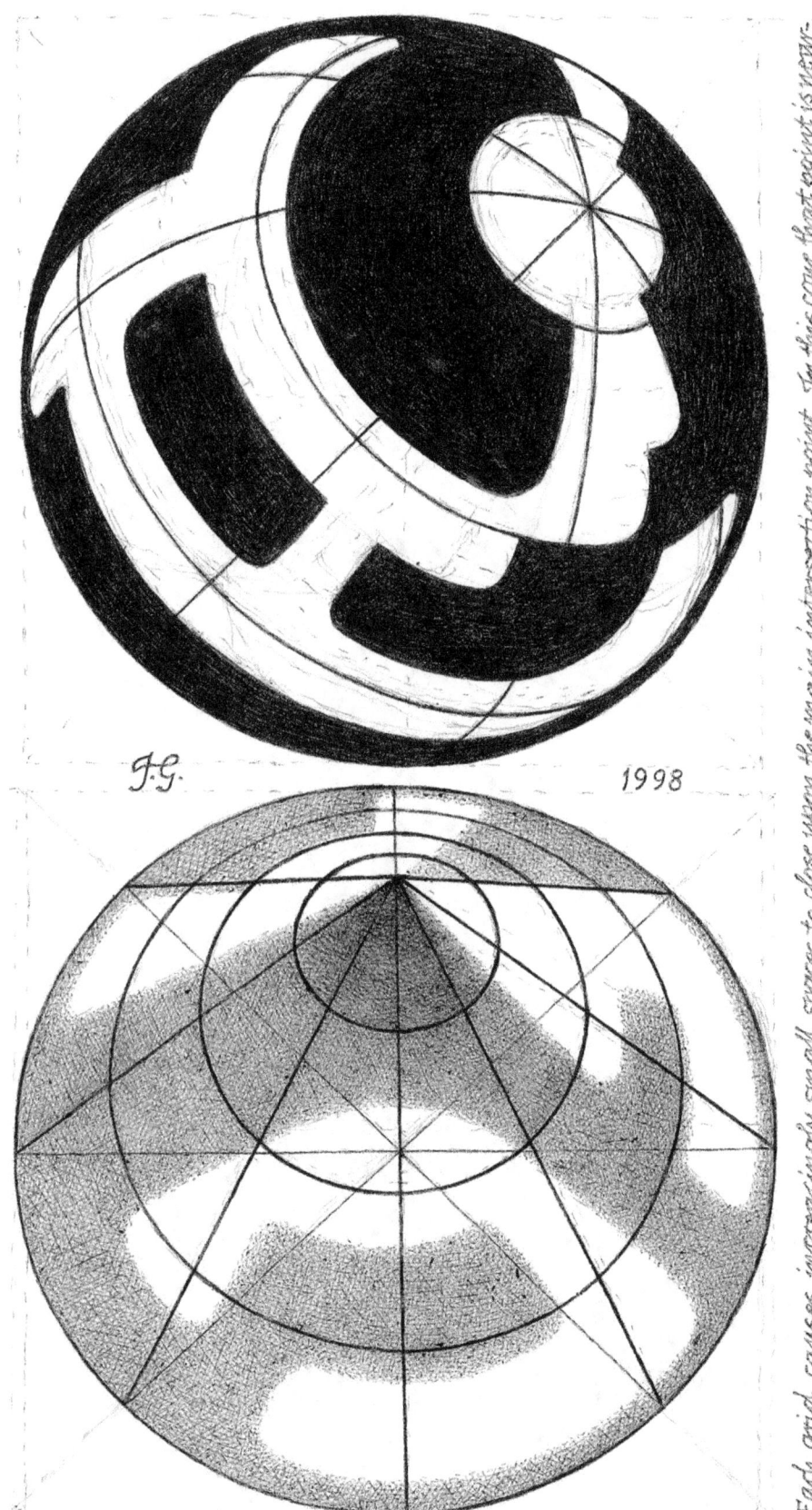

F.G.

1998

Each grid causes increasingly small spaces to close upon the main intersection point. In this case, that point is nearest to the viewer, while in a sphere the nearest place is always at the center of the circular outline. Yet, as designers, we may emphatically enlarge & heighten the shape displayed around either intersection. In the sphere this will mean that we do bring into direct contact with the viewer a most telling though not the nearest feature. In the cone, however, the actually most near & also characteristic part is emphatically the apex & should be so described. It is of import that the shrinking spaces of these grids are not intended as a guide to an equal descriptive diminution.

PLATE 44

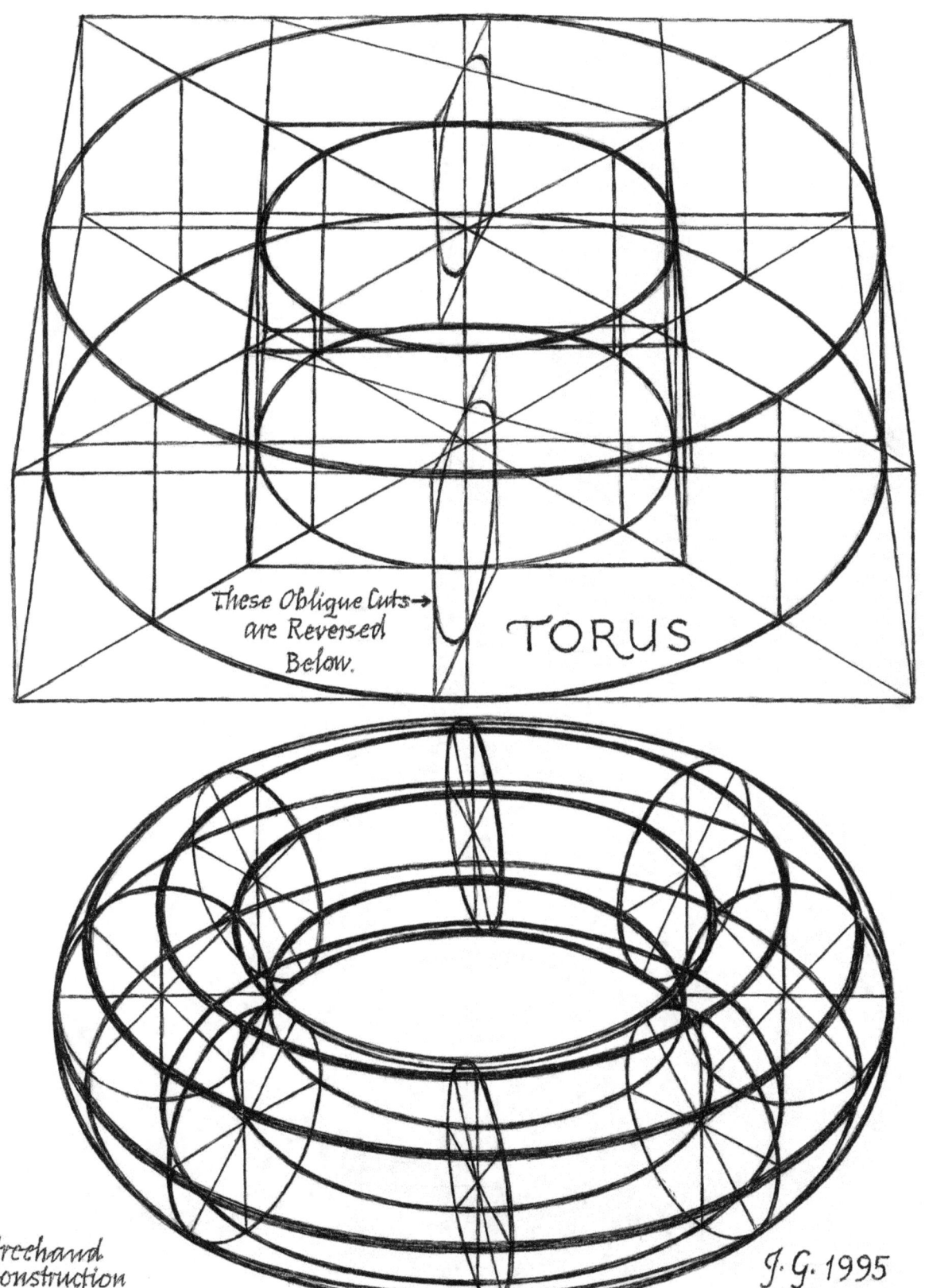

These Oblique Cuts → are Reversed Below.

TORUS

freehand Construction

J. G. 1995

PLATE 45

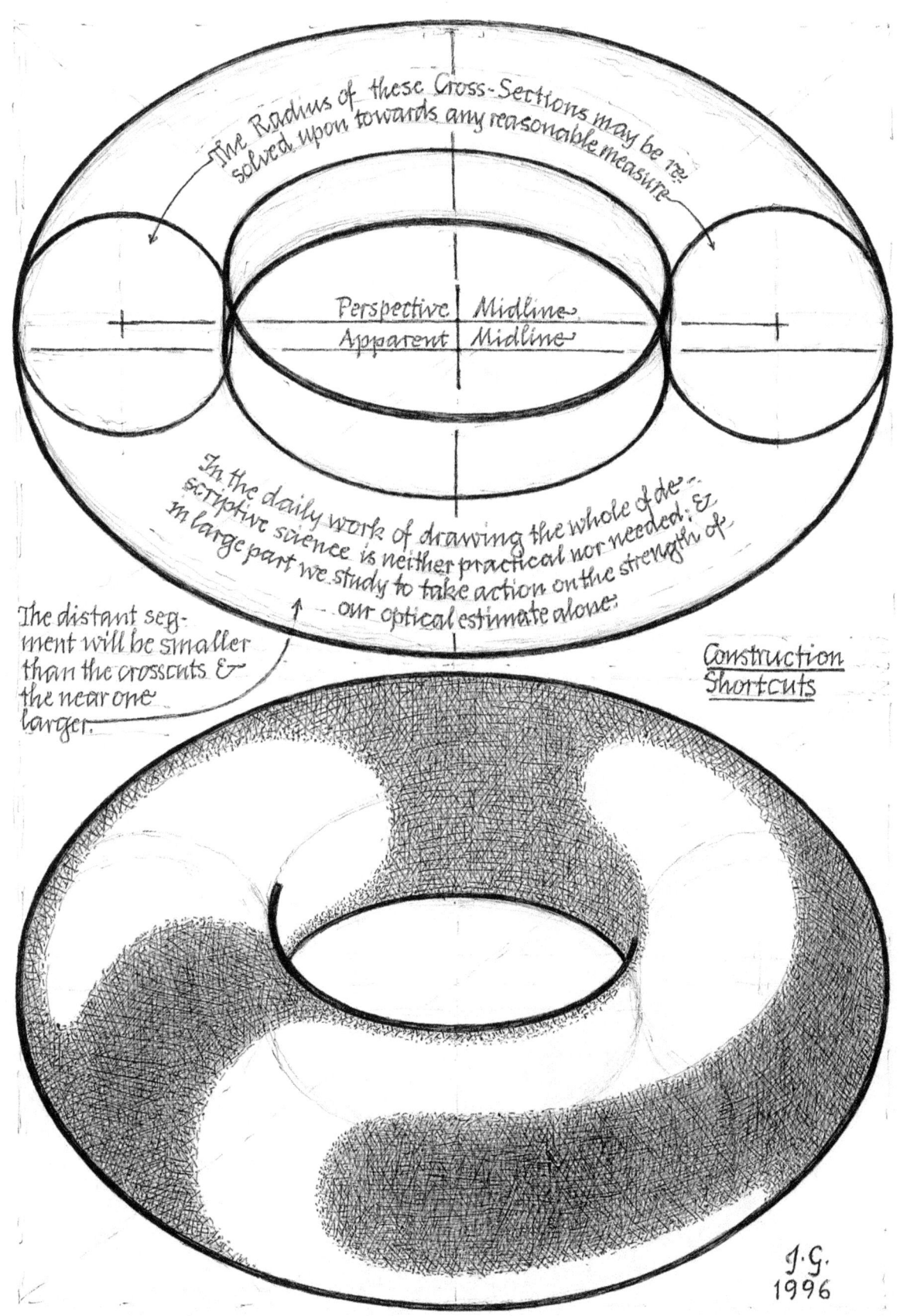

The Radius of these Cross-Sections may be re-solved upon towards any reasonable measure

| Perspective | Midline |
|---|---|
| Apparent | Midline |

In the daily work of drawing the whole of de-scriptive science is neither practical nor needed; & in large part we study to take action on the strength of our optical estimate alone.

The distant seg-ment will be smaller than the crosscuts & the near one larger.

Construction Shortcuts

J.G.
1996

PLATE 46

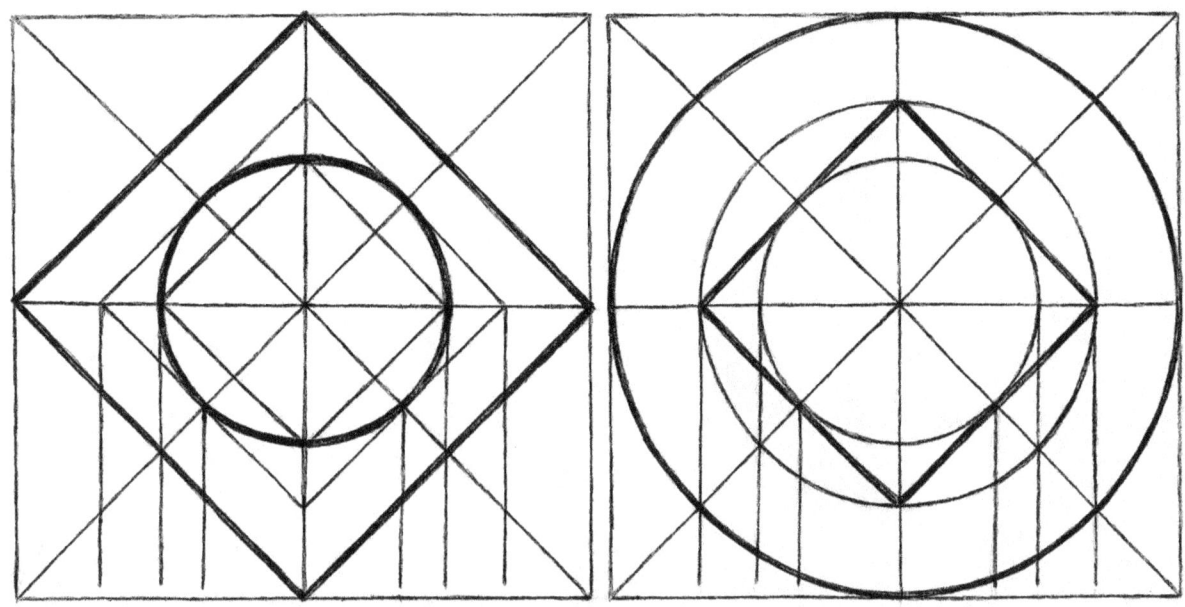

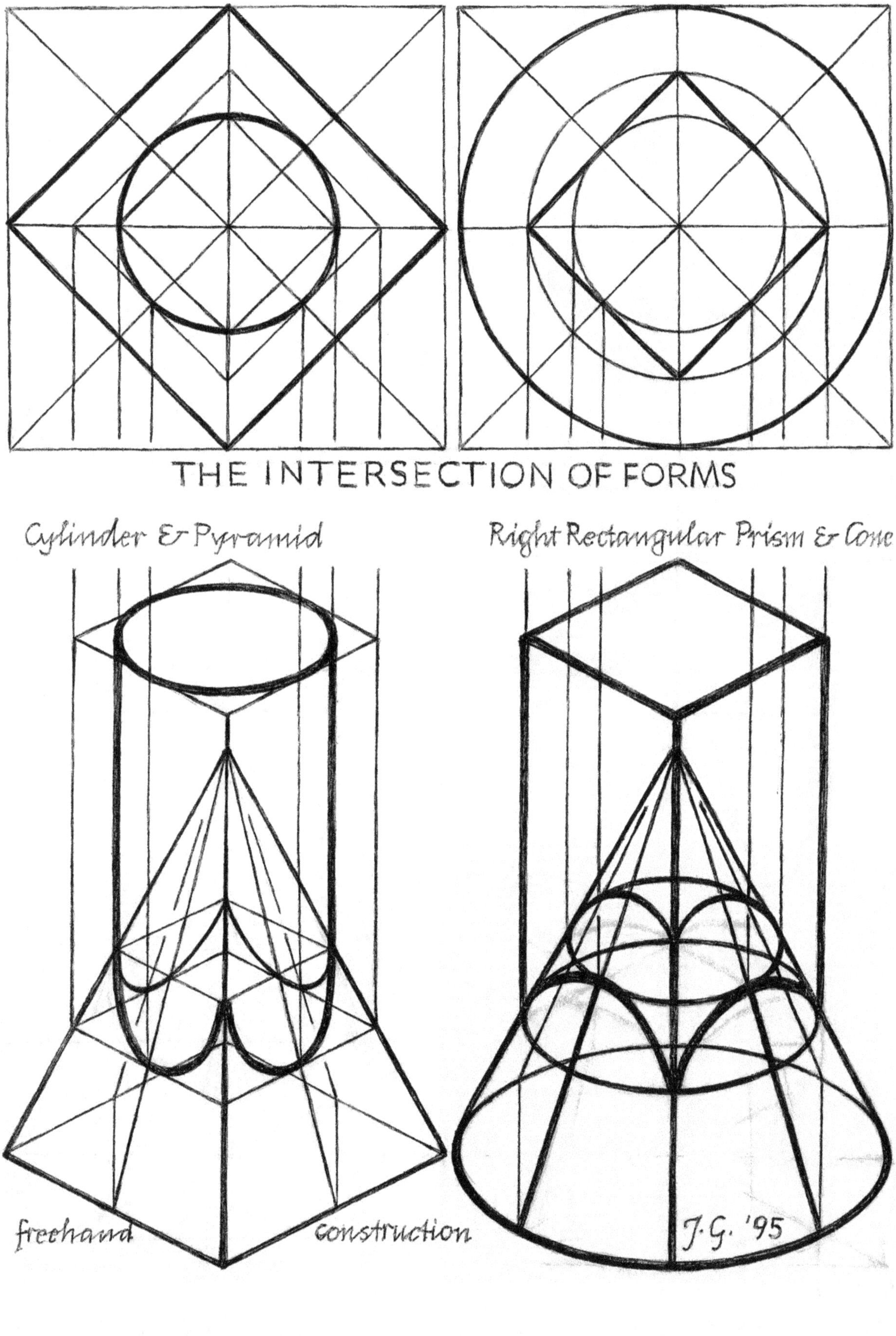

# THE INTERSECTION OF FORMS

*Cylinder & Pyramid*

*Right Rectangular Prism & Cone*

*freehand          construction*

*J·G· '95*

*PLATE 47*

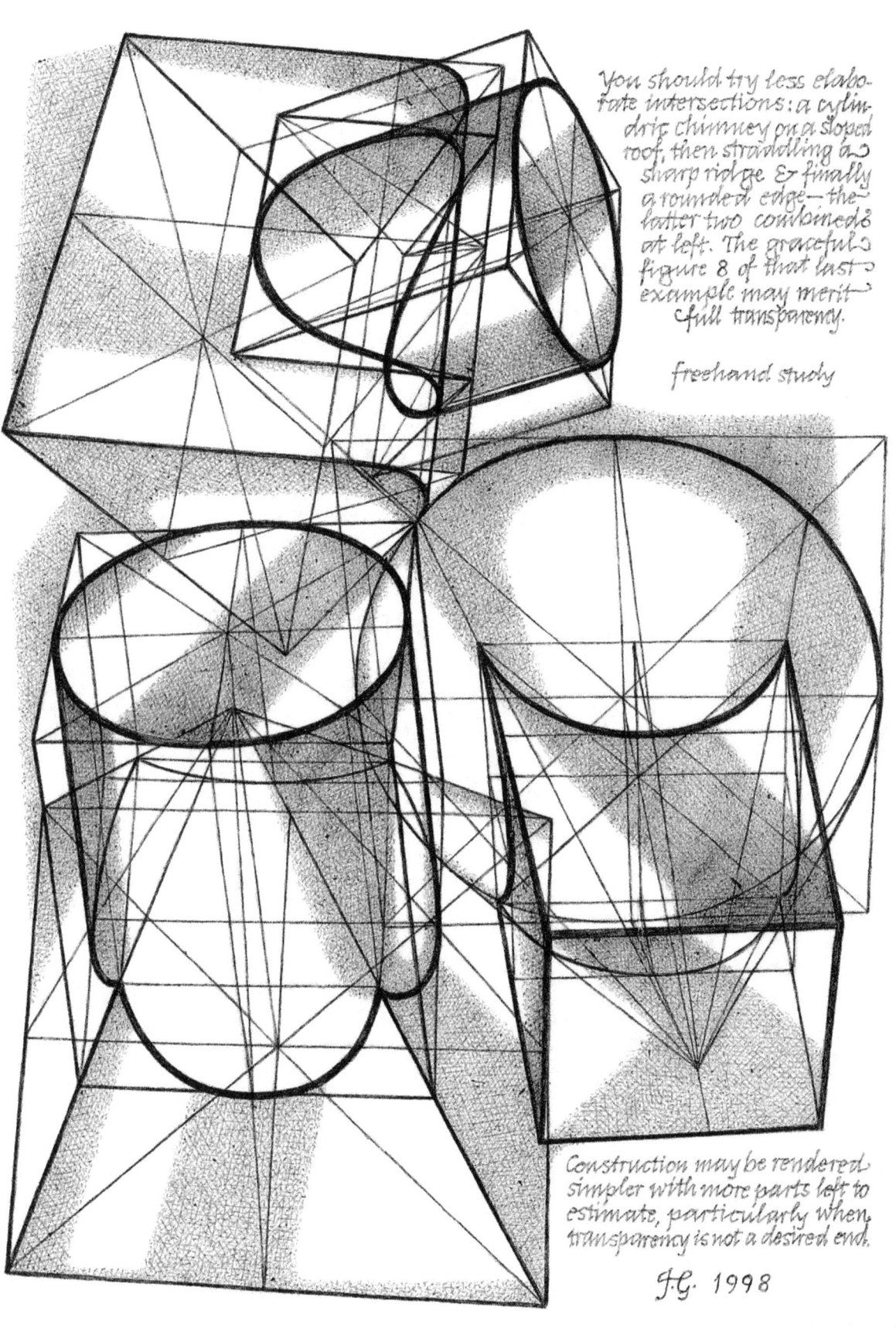

You should try less elaborate intersections: a cylindric chimney on a sloped roof, then straddling a sharp ridge & finally a rounded edge—the latter two combined at left. The graceful figure 8 of that last example may merit full transparency.

freehand study

Construction may be rendered simpler with more parts left to estimate, particularly when transparency is not a desired end.

JG 1998

*PLATE 48*

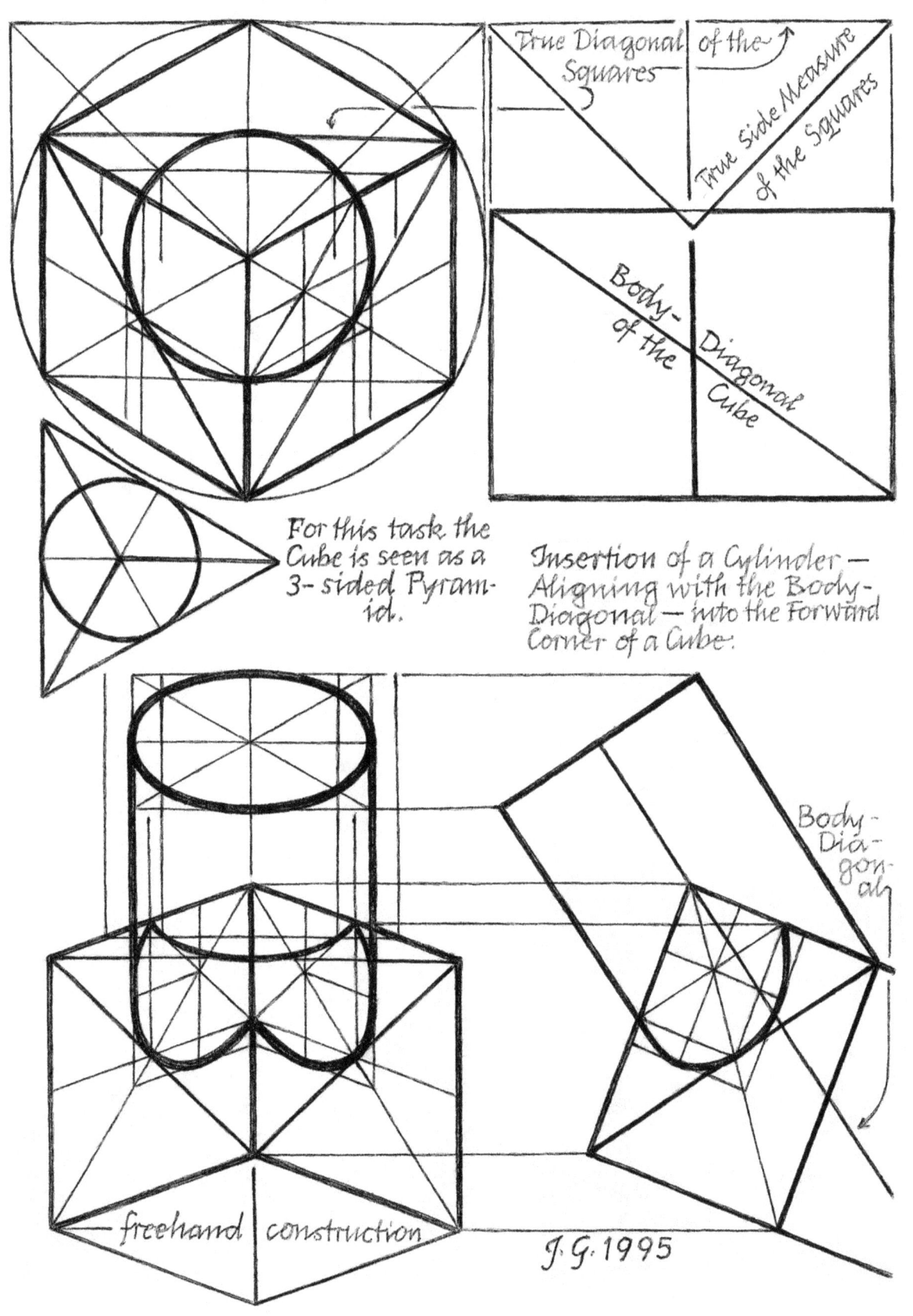

True Diagonal of the Squares

True Side Measure of the Squares

Body-Diagonal of the Cube

For this task the Cube is seen as a 3-sided Pyramid.

Insertion of a Cylinder — Aligning with the Body-Diagonal — into the Forward Corner of a Cube:

Body-Diagonal

freehand construction

J.G. 1995

PLATE 49

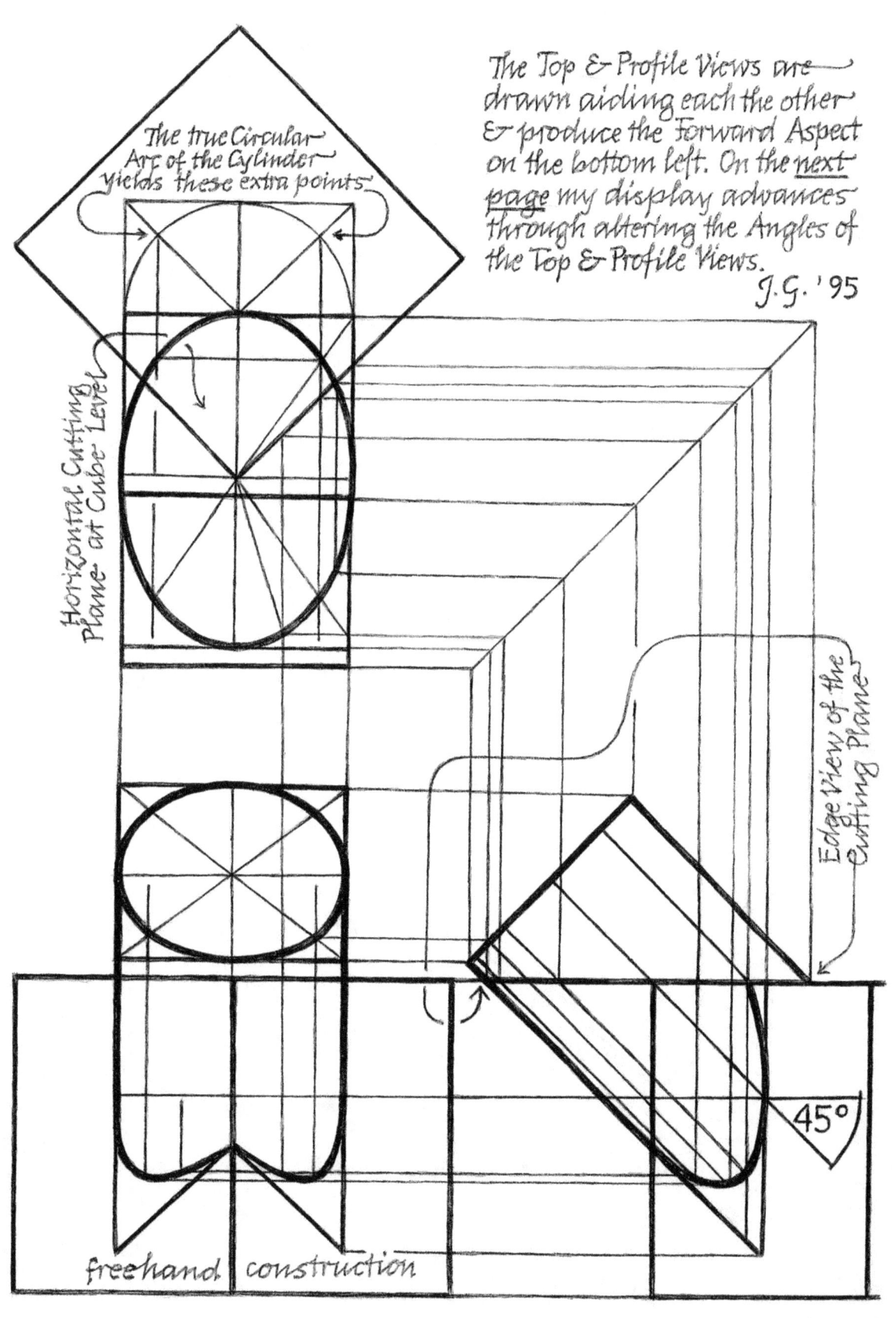

The true Circular Arc of the Cylinder yields these extra points

The Top & Profile Views are drawn aiding each the other & produce the Forward Aspect on the bottom left. On the <u>next page</u> my display advances through altering the Angles of the Top & Profile Views.

J.G. '95

Horizontal Cutting Plane at Cube Level

Edge View of the Cutting Plane

45°

freehand construction

PLATE 50

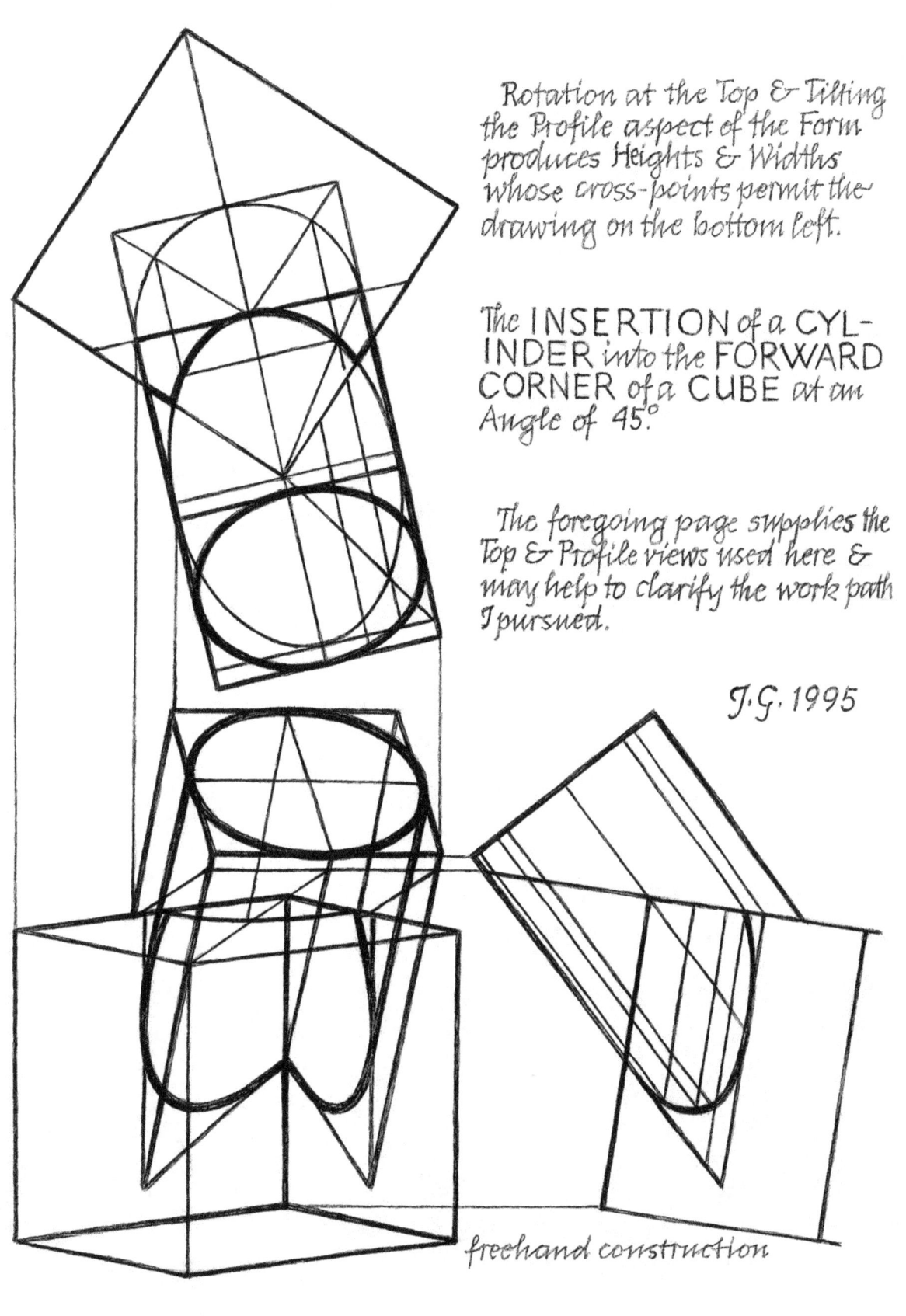

Rotation at the Top & Tilting the Profile aspect of the Form produces Heights & Widths whose cross-points permit the drawing on the bottom left.

The INSERTION of a CYLINDER into the FORWARD CORNER of a CUBE at an Angle of 45°.

The foregoing page supplies the Top & Profile views used here & may help to clarify the work path I pursued.

J·G· 1995

freehand construction

*PLATE 51*

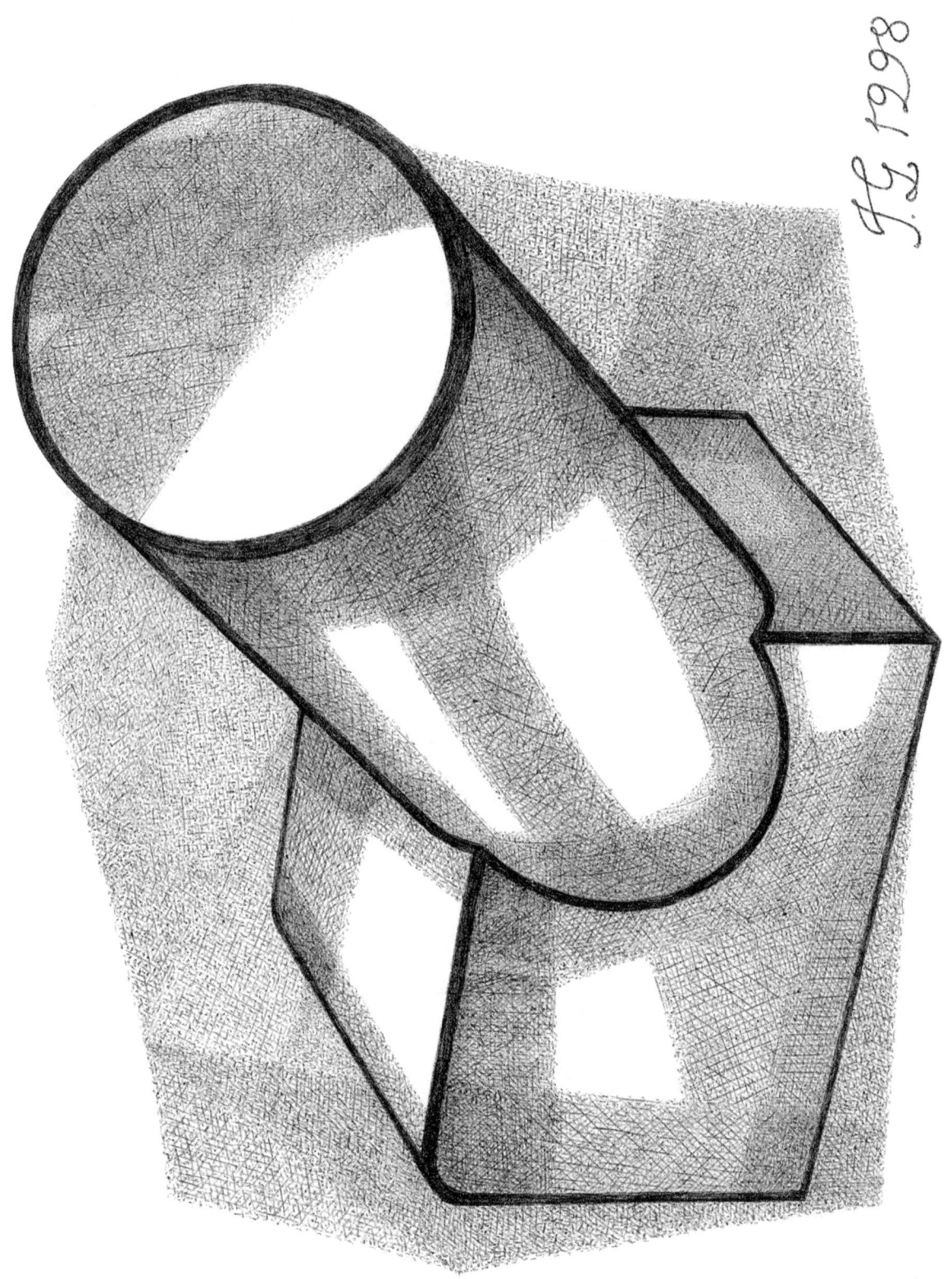

JG 1998

PLATE 52

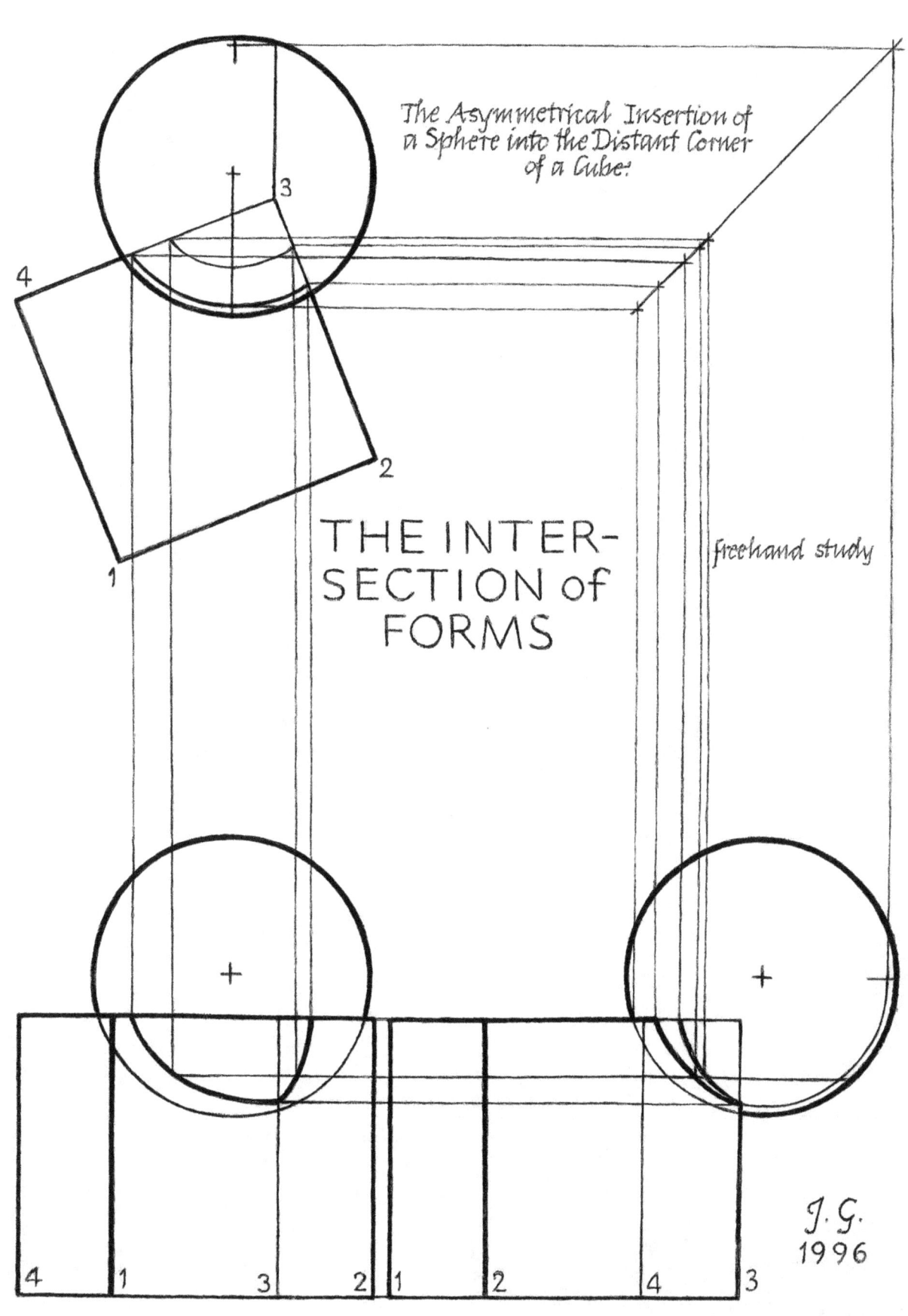

The Asymmetrical Insertion of
a Sphere into the Distant Corner
of a Cube:

THE INTER-
SECTION of
FORMS

*freehand study*

J.G.
1996

PLATE 53

The play of light is varied, but all the shapes it makes have a trait in common. This trait is the accord of every element to the geometry of forms, so that any geometric parts of our own design can describe with equal clarity.

But a rule for showing form in all the rays that we may want touches also that we are able to desire only what we can imagine; and this, all by itself, will be a finite reservoir indeed.

Light paints subtly a far richer shape array than the well-worn blending of shade & illuminated segments. Such subtleties are seldom visible to the untutored eye but can be discerned, intensified & re-composed in a wealth of variation our limited imaginings

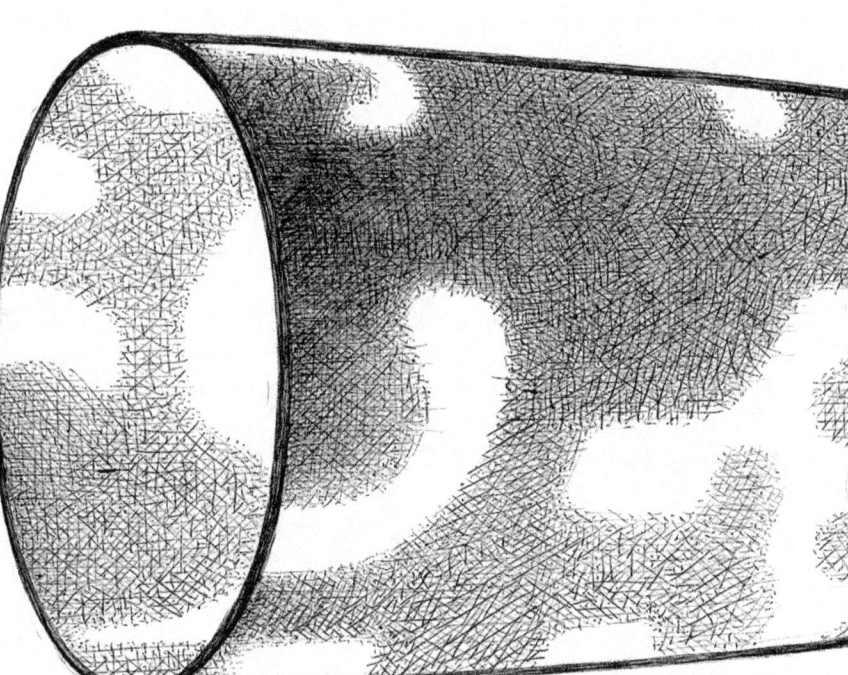

alone cannot bring forth.

Thus we go to nature—not to copy what she readily reveals—but to build for ourselves a storehouse of configurations we are not on our own able even to desire.

Through strengthening & co-herently re-organizing what we have observed we carry out the artist's task of surpassing the material prototype—of creating better than his subject.

This drawing, it is hoped, may thus engage the viewer more persuasively than the vaguely white, translucent plastic cup that supplied the model.

J.G. 1997

PLATE 54

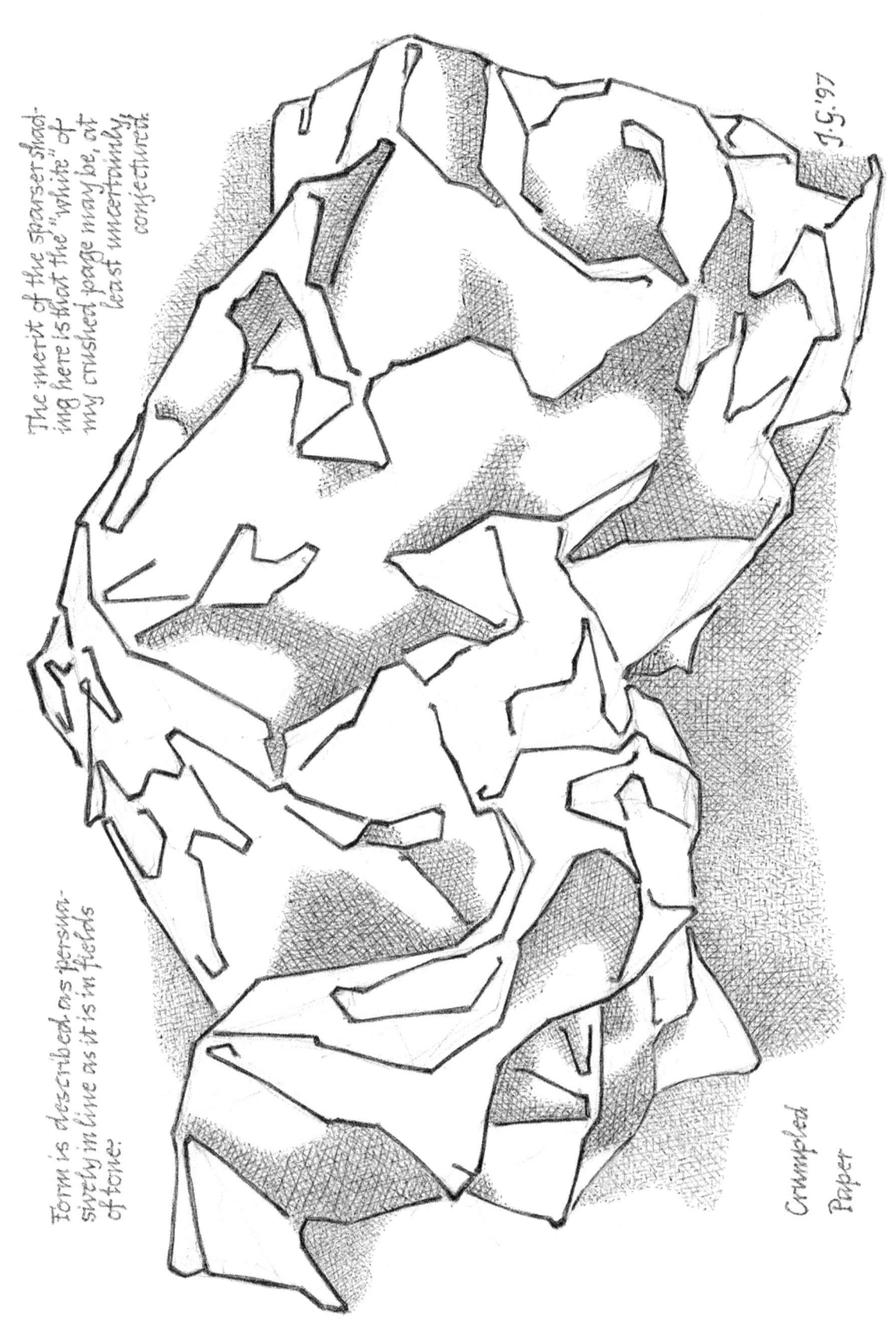

The merit of the sparser shading here is that the "white" of
my crushed page may be, at
least uncertainly,
conjectural.

J.G. '97

Form is described as persuasively in line as it is in fields
of tone.

Crumpled
Paper

*PLATE 55*

Always, in ordinary drawing, we repeat this action: We first look at our object and then upon the page while laying down what we suppose we saw as best we can remember.

# In CONTOUR DRAWING the artist only sees his page each time he sets his tool to give himself a start but never when it is in motion.

Contour Drawing is extremely useful as the most acutely concentrated means for observing and recording the detailed peculiarities of forms and one of our sharpest tools for exercising our drawing hand.

The results are often so engaging, we balk at acknowleging their limitations: However, they seldom deliver exactitude of structure & proportion. By nearly always looking at the object but rarely at the drawing surface, the artist may not succeed entirely at his task of page design. Thus the craft of fashioning this product is not wholly our own. Instead its beauty is a gift to us from a particular technique and not any due reward for our skill & talent.

J.G.

1998

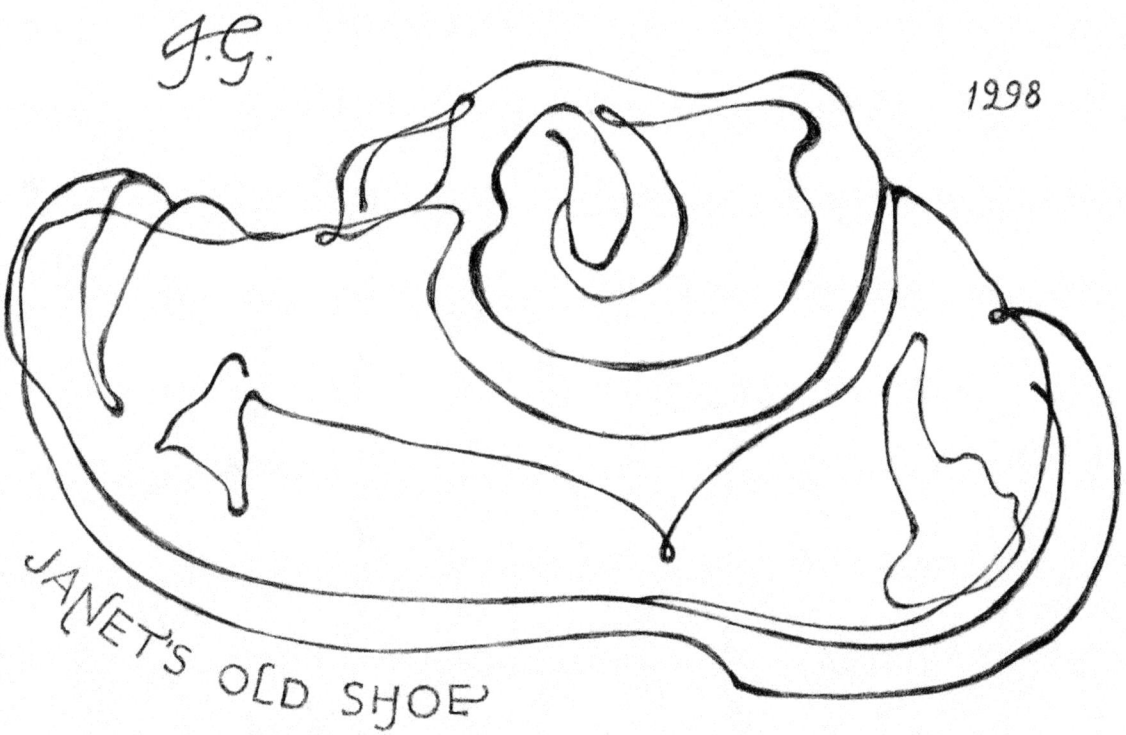

JANET'S OLD SHOE

After all the contours are in place, we may use a varied weight of stroke to accent attributes of import as well as those of special personal appeal.

PLATE 56

In any truly exacting work of observation Nature is able to surprise & delight us through disclosing her most elusive surface features in renderable, telling shape & clean-cut line. These features are Nature's open secrets; & she readily reveals them to sharp eyes & willing minds.

J.G. 1998

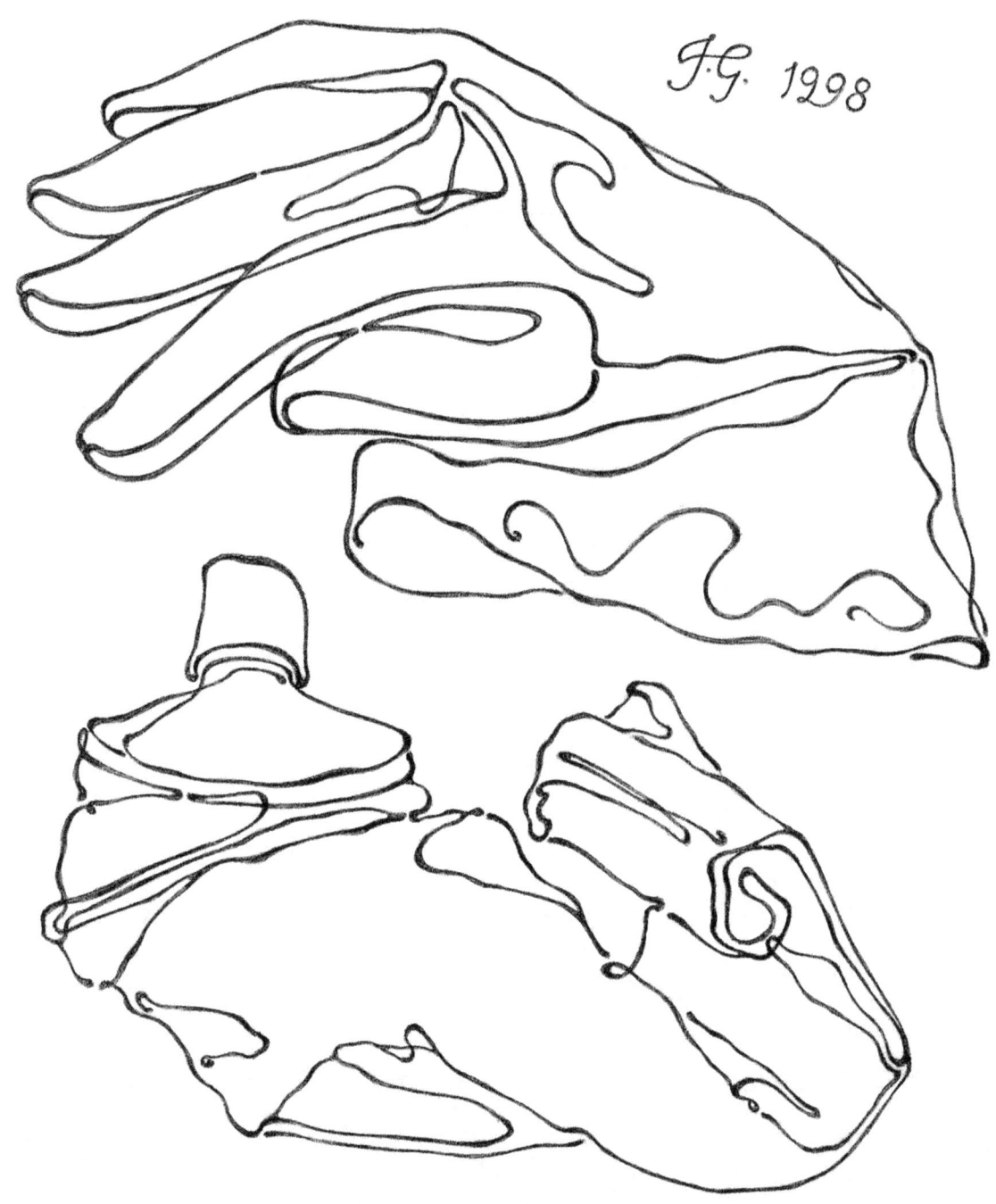

The drawings here are traced & hence adjusted to the page with care. This made possible improvements in their individual designs. But it brought besides slight weakening in the earlier sense of immediate, all but tangible engagement with the object.

PLATE 57

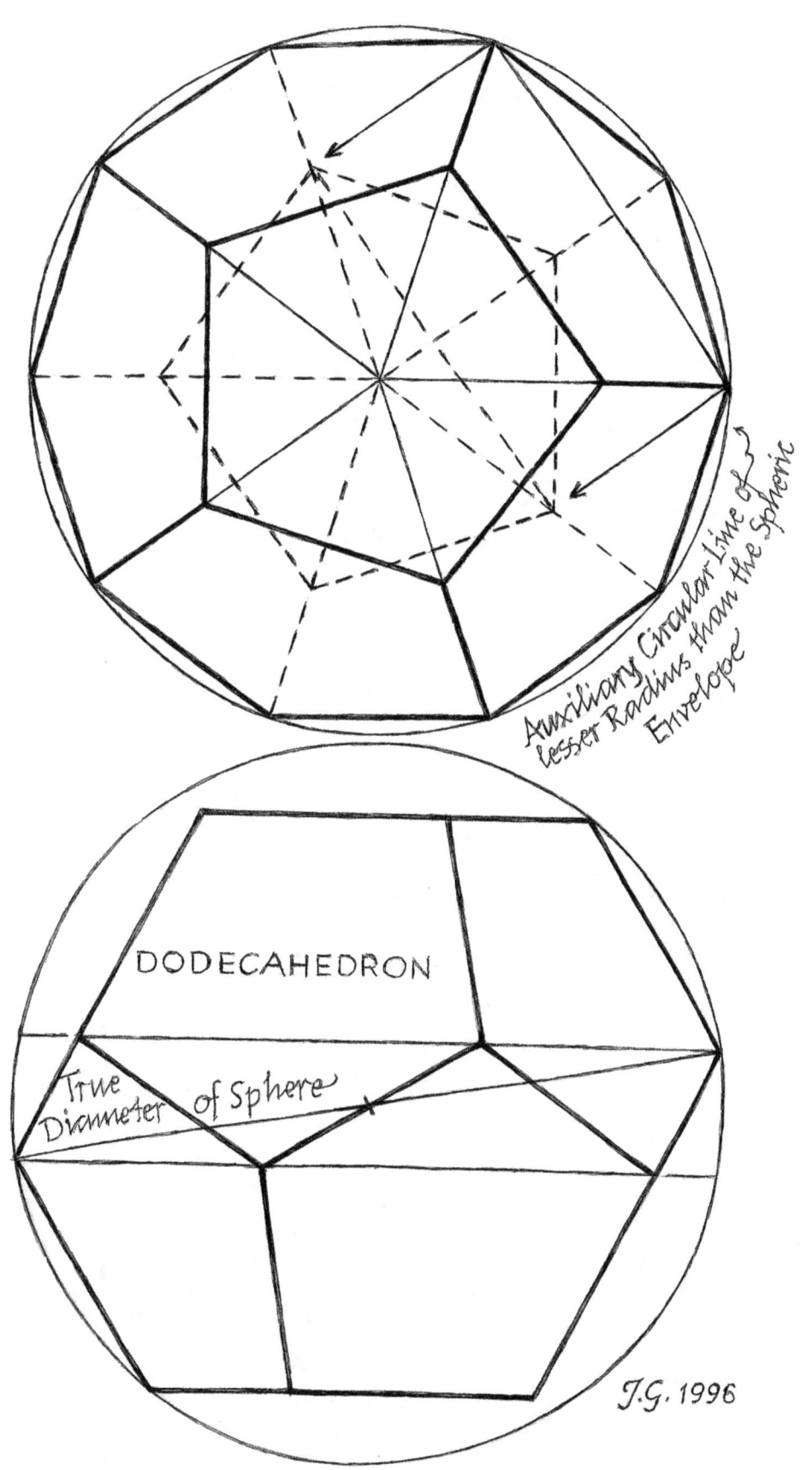

Auxiliary Circular Line of lesser Radius than the Spheric Envelope

DODECAHEDRON

True Diameter of Sphere

J.G. 1996

PLATE 58

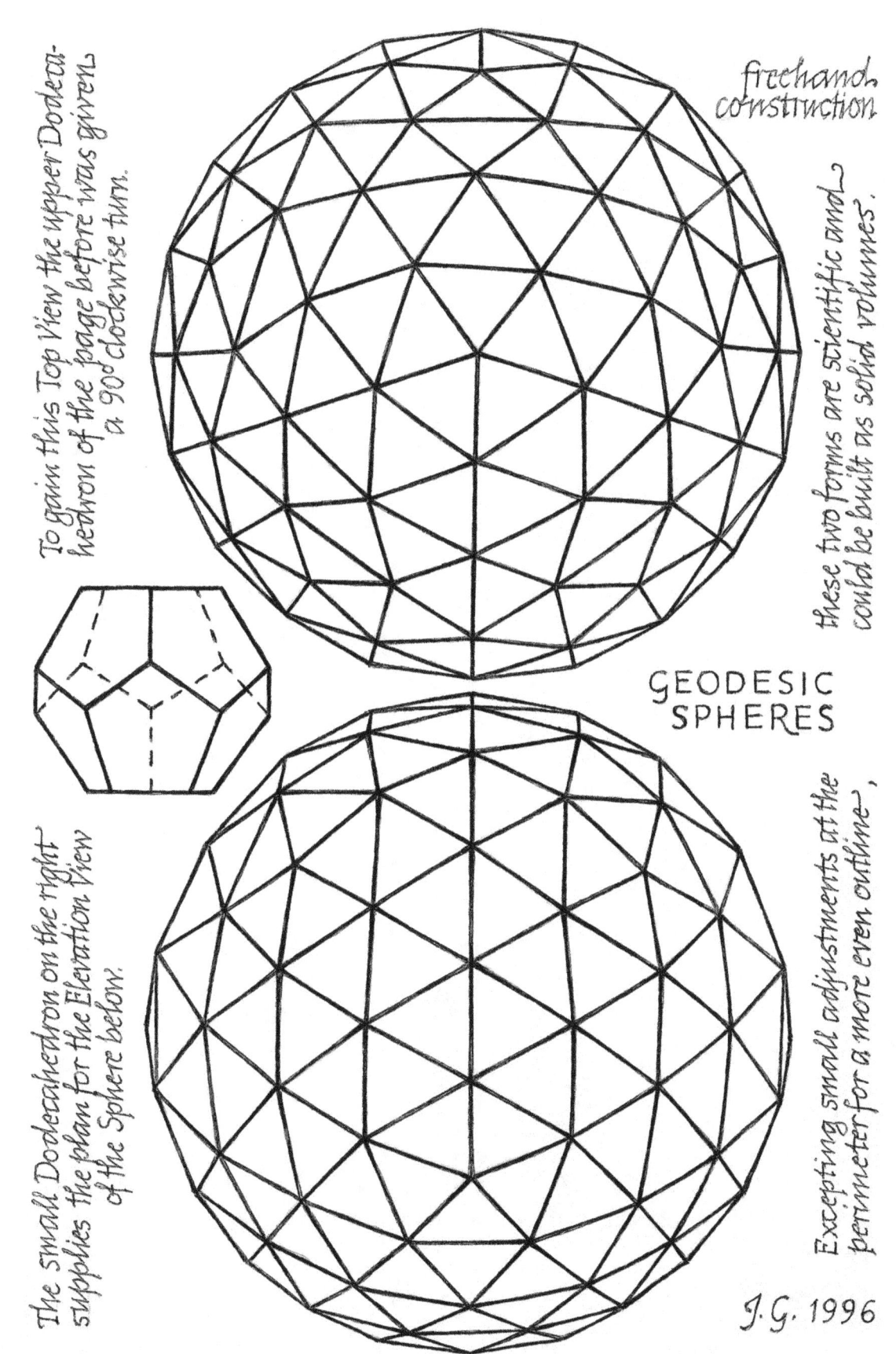

freehand
construction

To gain this Top View the upper Dodecahedron of the page before was given
a 90° clockwise turn.

these two forms are scientific and
could be built as solid volumes.

GEODESIC
SPHERES

The small Dodecahedron on the right
supplies the plan for the Elevation View
of the Sphere below.

Excepting small adjustments at the
perimeter for a more even outline,

J. G. 1996

PLATE 59

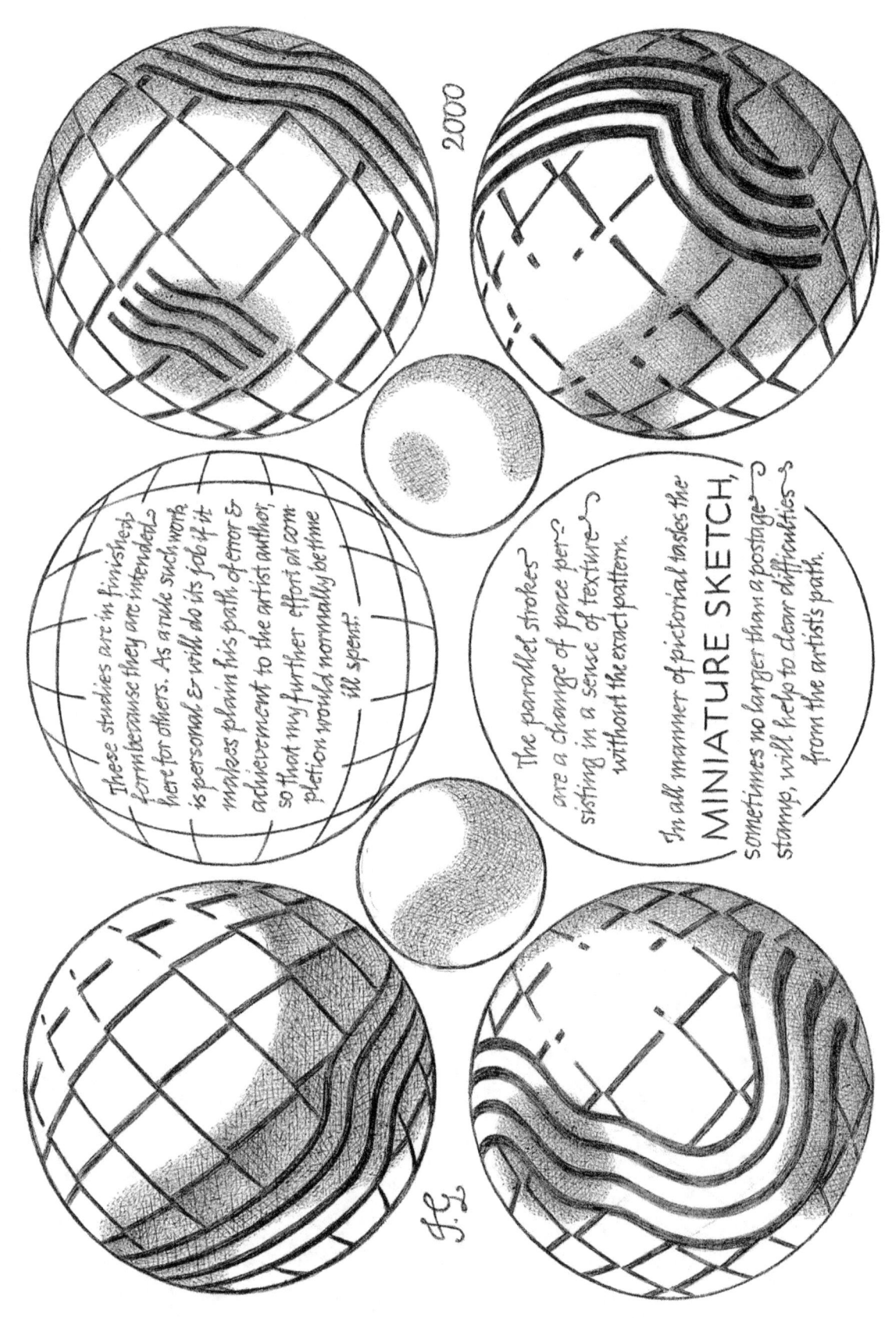

2000

These studies are in finished form because they are intended here for others. As a rule such work is personal & will do its job if it makes plain his path of error & achievement to the artist author, so that my further effort at completion would normally be time ill spent.

The parallel strokes are a change of pace persisting in a sense of texture without the exact pattern.

In all manner of pictorial tasks the MINIATURE SKETCH, sometimes no larger than a postage stamp, will help to clear difficulties from the artist's path.

PLATE 60

At right, unequal join-
ings of the parts convey
the form. But light &
shade are needed with
the angle of regard less
favorable. These at times
obscure details in cavities
while prominences be-
come clear.

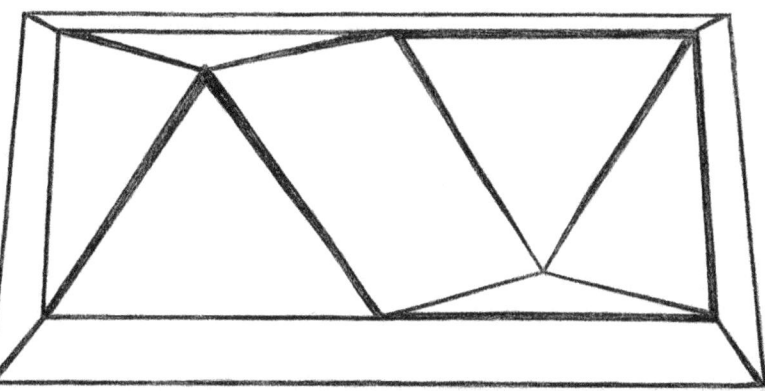

Light & shade can be implied by wheight of line. Thus my point at depth is most

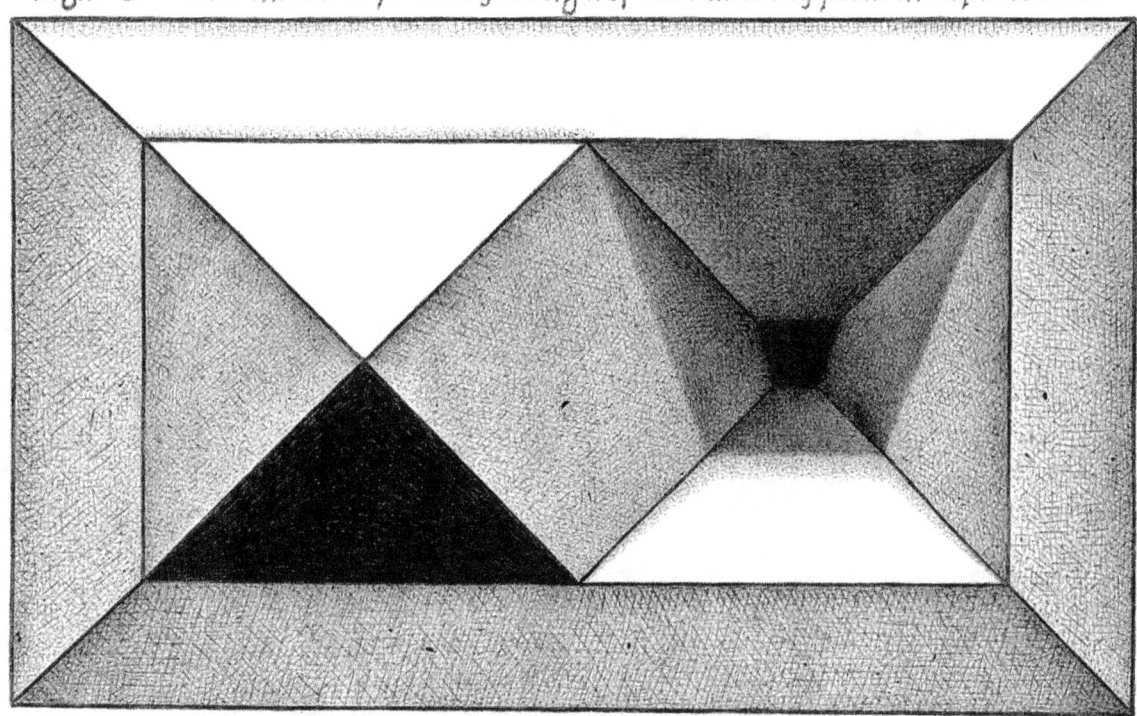

times finely drawn & that at peak in bolder strokes.

Compare the flattening of
the untreated line below
with the effects of varied
line at left.

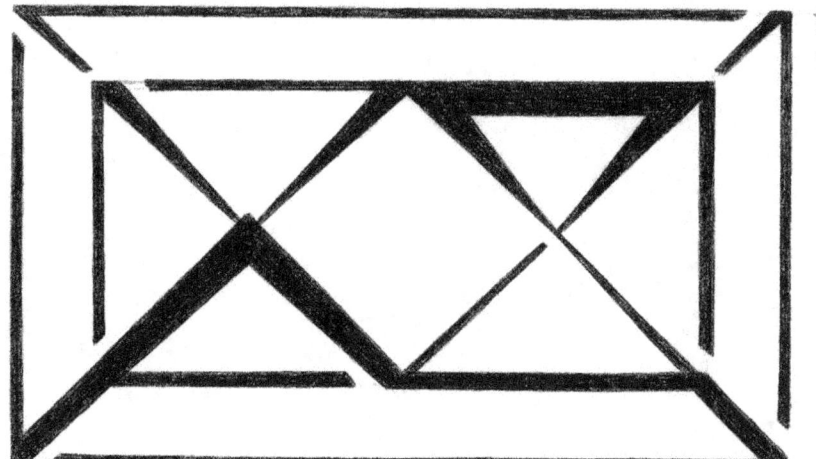

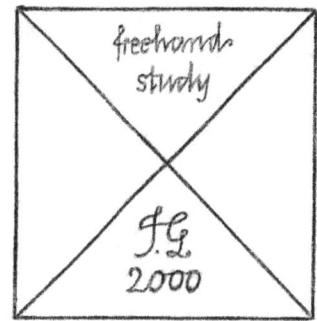

freehand
study

J.G.
2000

PLATE 61

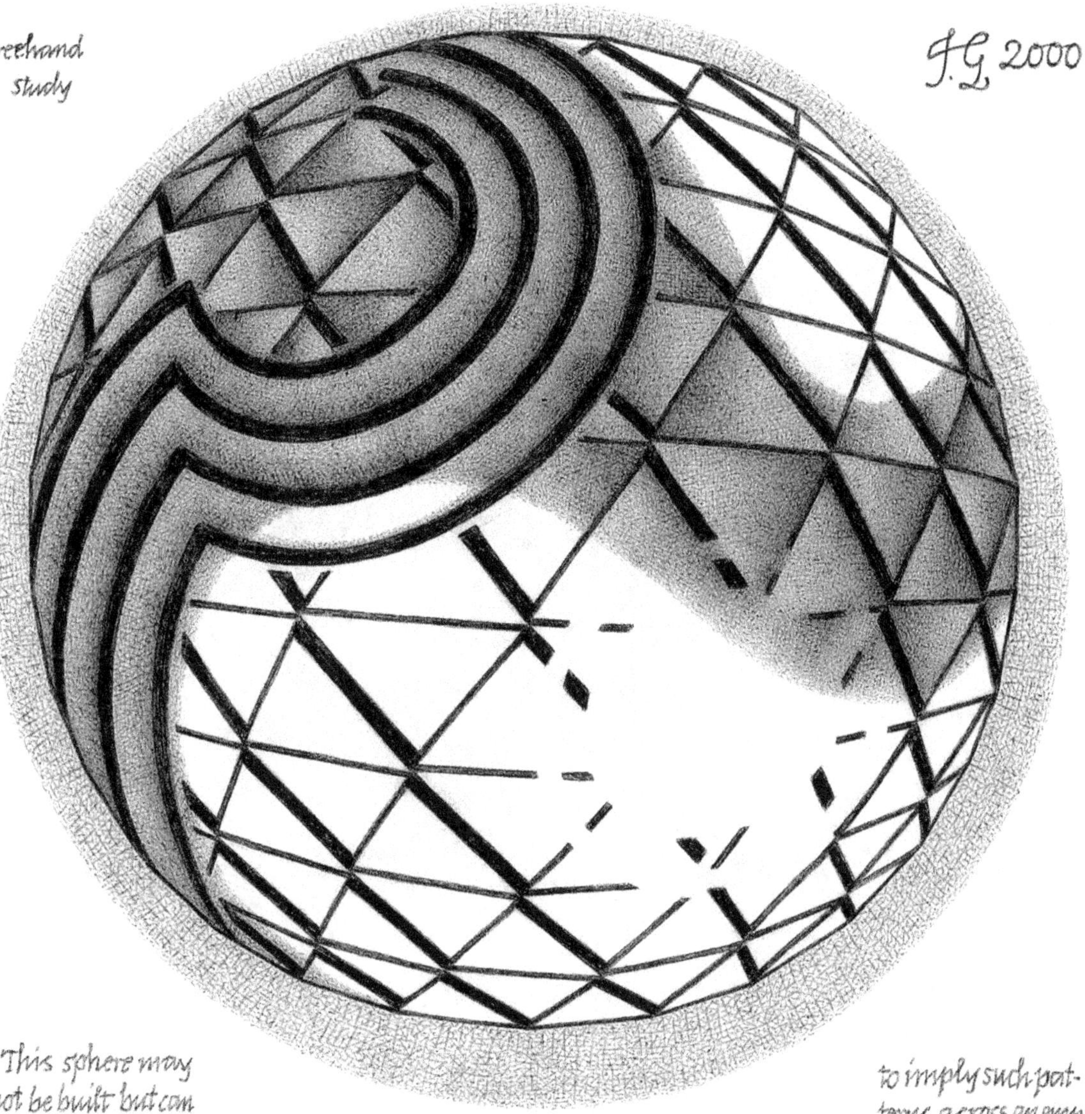

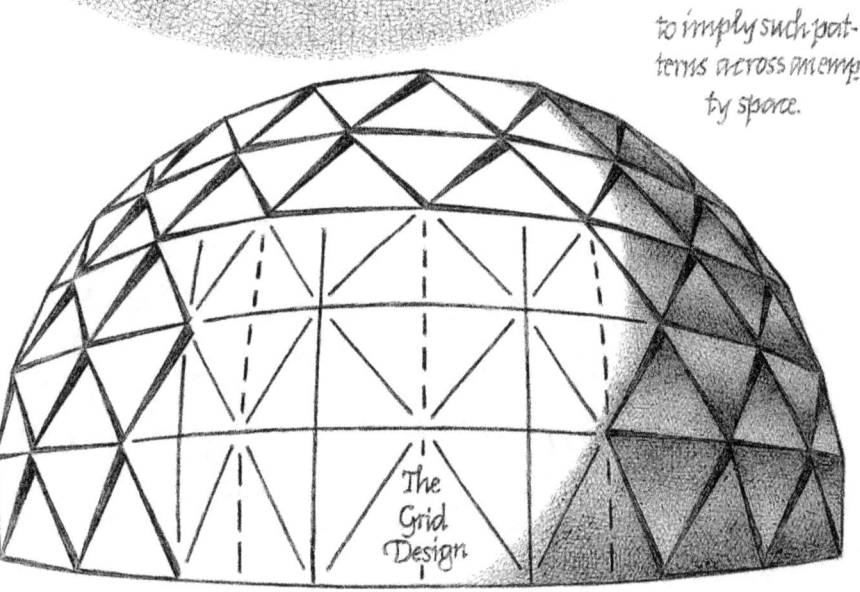

This sphere may not be built but can be drawn & seen.

Outlines are here shaped to sharpen corners.

Shading sharpens edges, so that my solid will not be turned into a cavity through obscuring of the pattern.

One or two graduated steps may help to imply such patterns across an empty space.

The Grid Design

PLATE 62

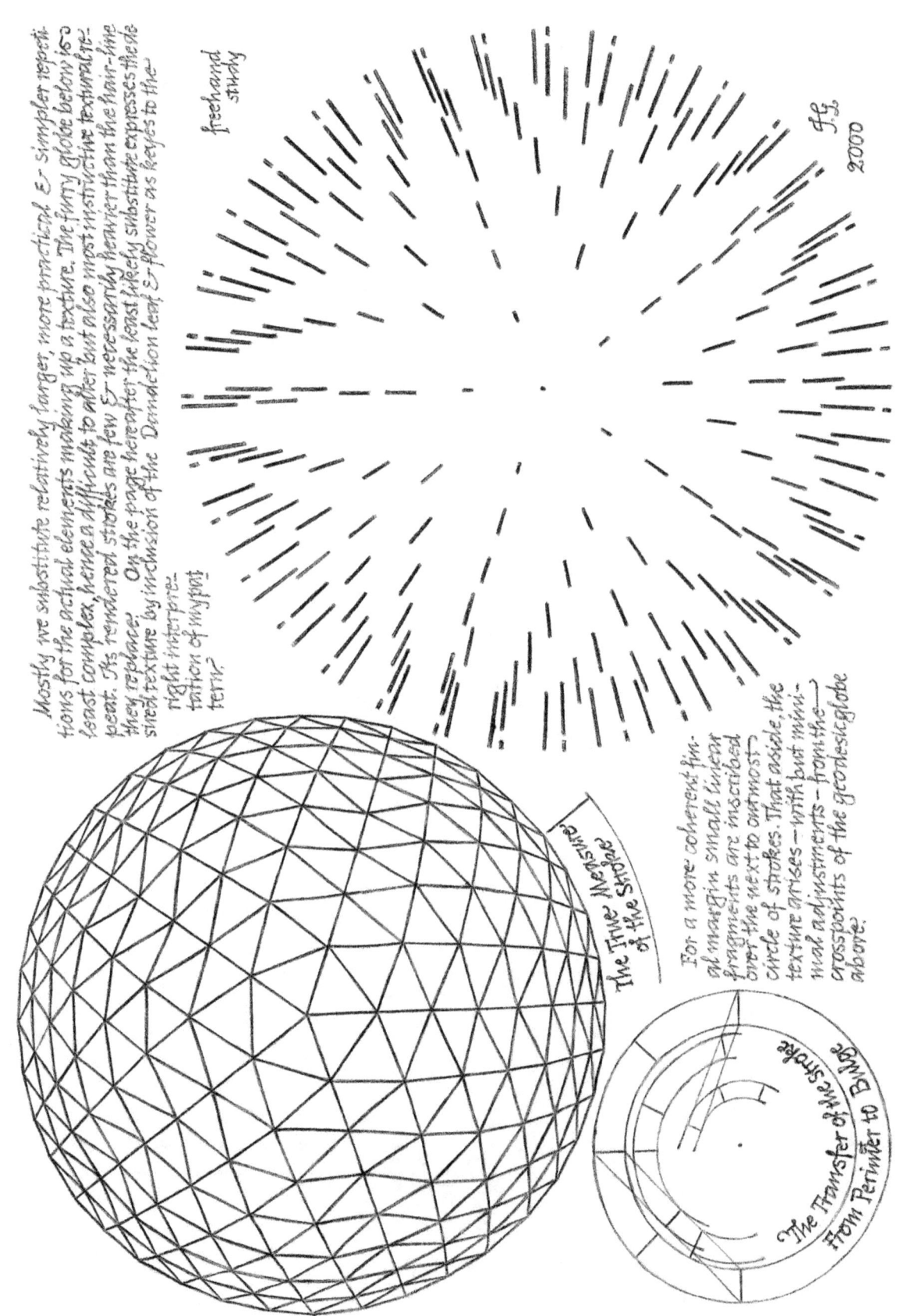

Mostly we substitute relatively larger, more practical & simpler repetitions for the actual elements making up a texture. The furry globe below is a least complex, hence a difficult to alter but also most instructive textural repeat. Its rendered strokes are few & necessarily heavier than the hair-line they replace. On the page hereafter the least likely substitute expresses these single texture by inclusion of the Demolition leaf & flower as keyes to the right interpretation of my pattern.

freehand study

f.g. 2000

The True Measure of the Strokes

For a more coherent finial margin small linear fragments are inscribed over the next to outmost circle of strokes. That aside, the texture arises—with but minimal adjustments—from the crosspoints of the geodesic globe above.

The Transfer of the Stroke
From Perimeter to Bundle

PLATE 63

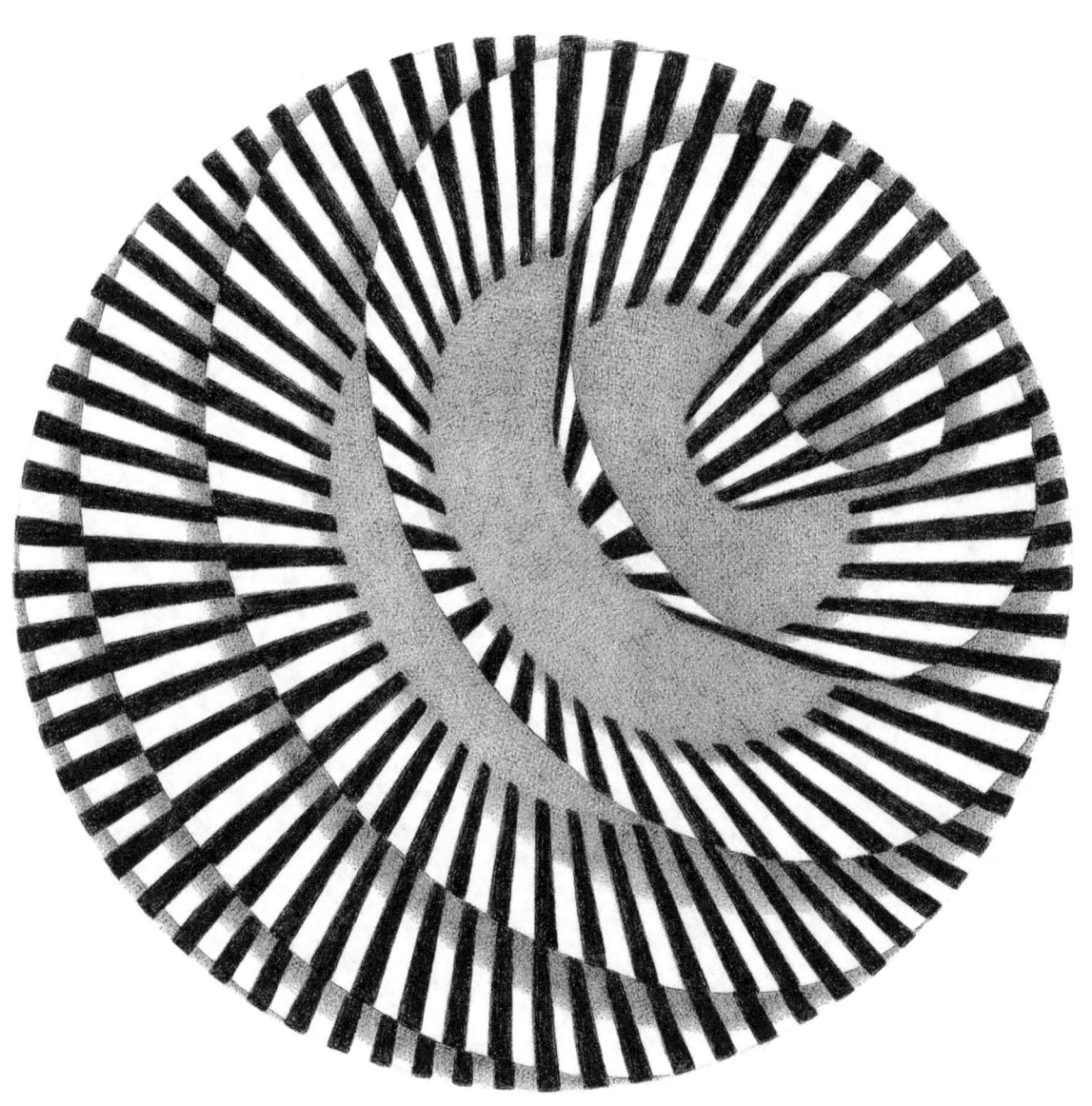

To see sculpture & to find it excellent the beholder assembles his eventual overall
impression from at least subtly differing aspects. The draftsman & the painter must
show volume solidly by composing an unalterable view, so that the created formal
product is not as such the object but the entire page or canvas where the work is done.

A manner of close kinship with the natural world may grant the artist in-
sufficient space of action to achieve this outcome excellently. Good design may
here demand, besides ability, an apt or lucky choice of theme.

This near trompe l'œil display may or may not give to me such luck. Mainly it
completes my assembly of discoveries which can link a drawing to real objects
of this kind. My entire table of such discoveries will be rendered on another page.

J. G. 2003

*PLATE 64*

1. We see the bristles of a Chestnut Burr emerging into light from surrounding dark. In the foregoing drawing the white spaces must carry out this action.

2. Also, in that drawing, each rank displaces at the edge completely the rank of strokes which follows. In nature this is not how that overlap occurs. Instead the outmost bristles, which alone are seen in their unforshortened measure, join with the first ones inward as a united pattern of a density that seemingly grows sparser toward center.

3. The look of the repeat at the perimeter is the main key for reading what kind of texture we behold.

4. In nature the bristles strive away from the global core. To link therefore the outer zig-zag spikes or single strokes to those within – letting an association by proximity join with our recall of experience – such textures appear never painted smoothly on the surface as we see them on the right. For they must lift off, at least to a degree, from the limits of the core.

5. The tilting of the object, which may show forshortened circular paths on which the textures travel or appear to travel, can serve to state the volume as a whole.

6. When a large part of a texture is obscured by tone the entire object tends to seem concave. Crisply separating lines shaping the volume overall can therefore serve the artist better; or tone may be used to describe such an object as a whole with texture showing only on the margin.

What we draw must never emphatically, that is, too visibly contradict these actualities. Yet rarely need an artist use every recognition signal known for any single work. Thus rendering abstractions which can make these forms & textures readable is a task we may very variously accomplish.

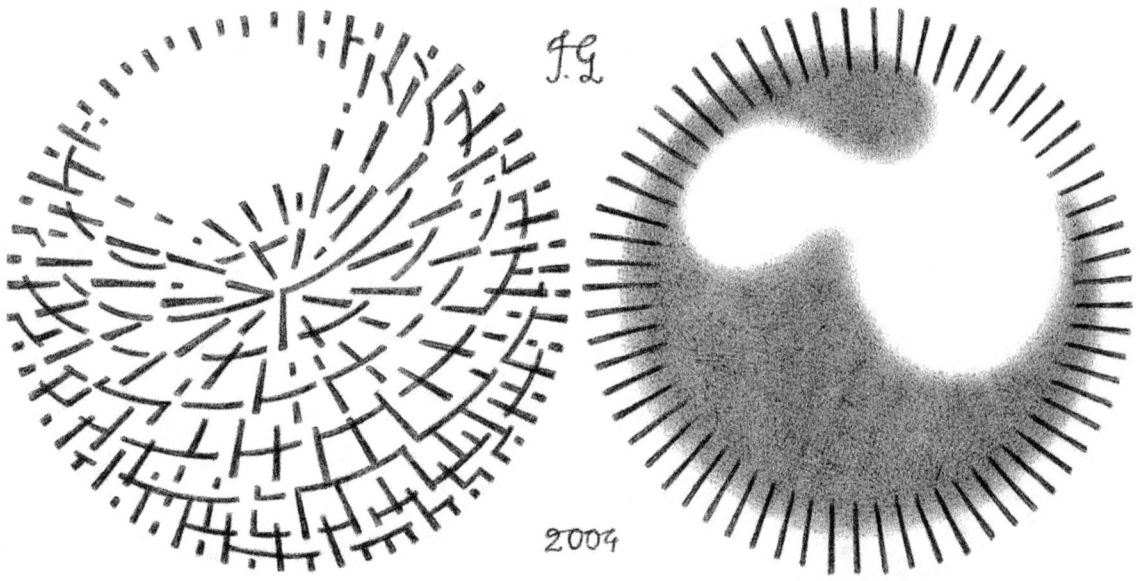

J.G.

2004

PLATE 65

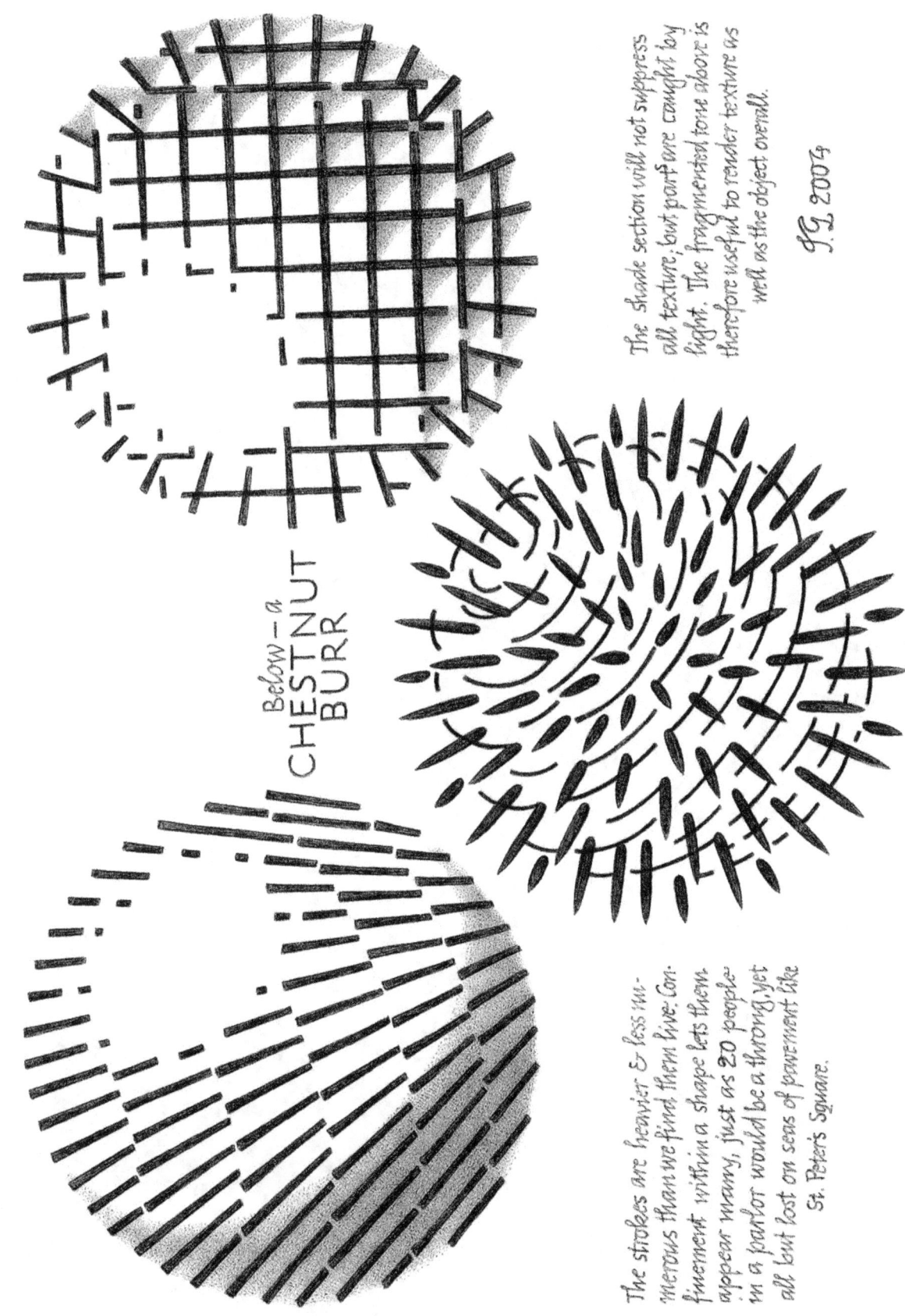

Below — a
CHESTNUT
BURR

The shade section will not suppress all texture; but part are caught by light. The fragmented tone above is therefore useful to render texture as well as the object overall.

JG 2004

The strokes are heavier & less numerous than we find them five. Confinement within a shape lets them appear many, just as 20 people in a parlor would be a throng, yet all but lost on seas of pavement like St. Peter's Square.

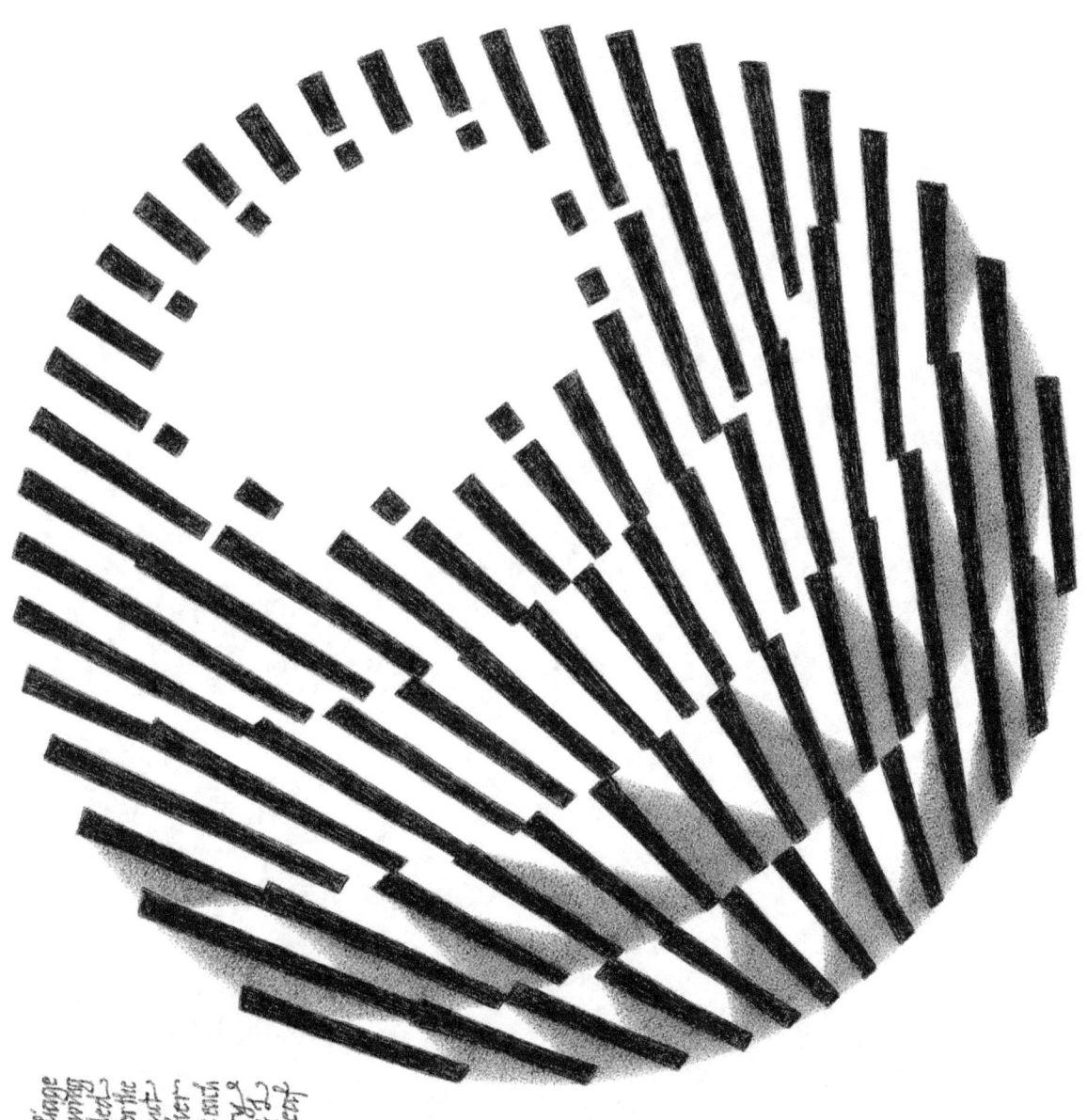

JG 2009

The elements of foliage on the page following is not much needed— there not helpful for the preceding Chestnut Burr. But my other attempts became each more fully a furry seed-head when I place a stem & leaf beneath.

PLATE 67

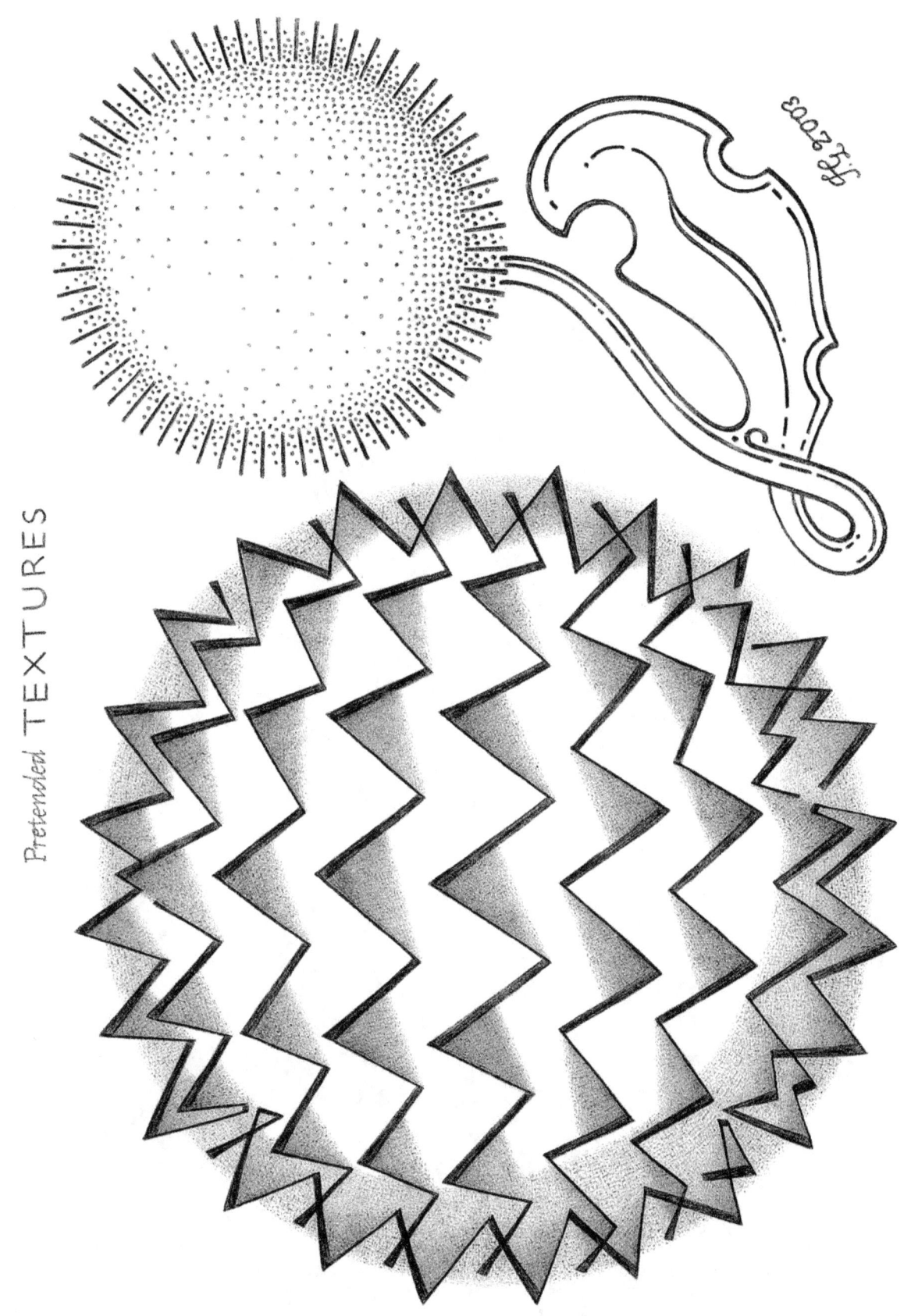

Pretended TEXTURES

ff 2003

PLATE 68

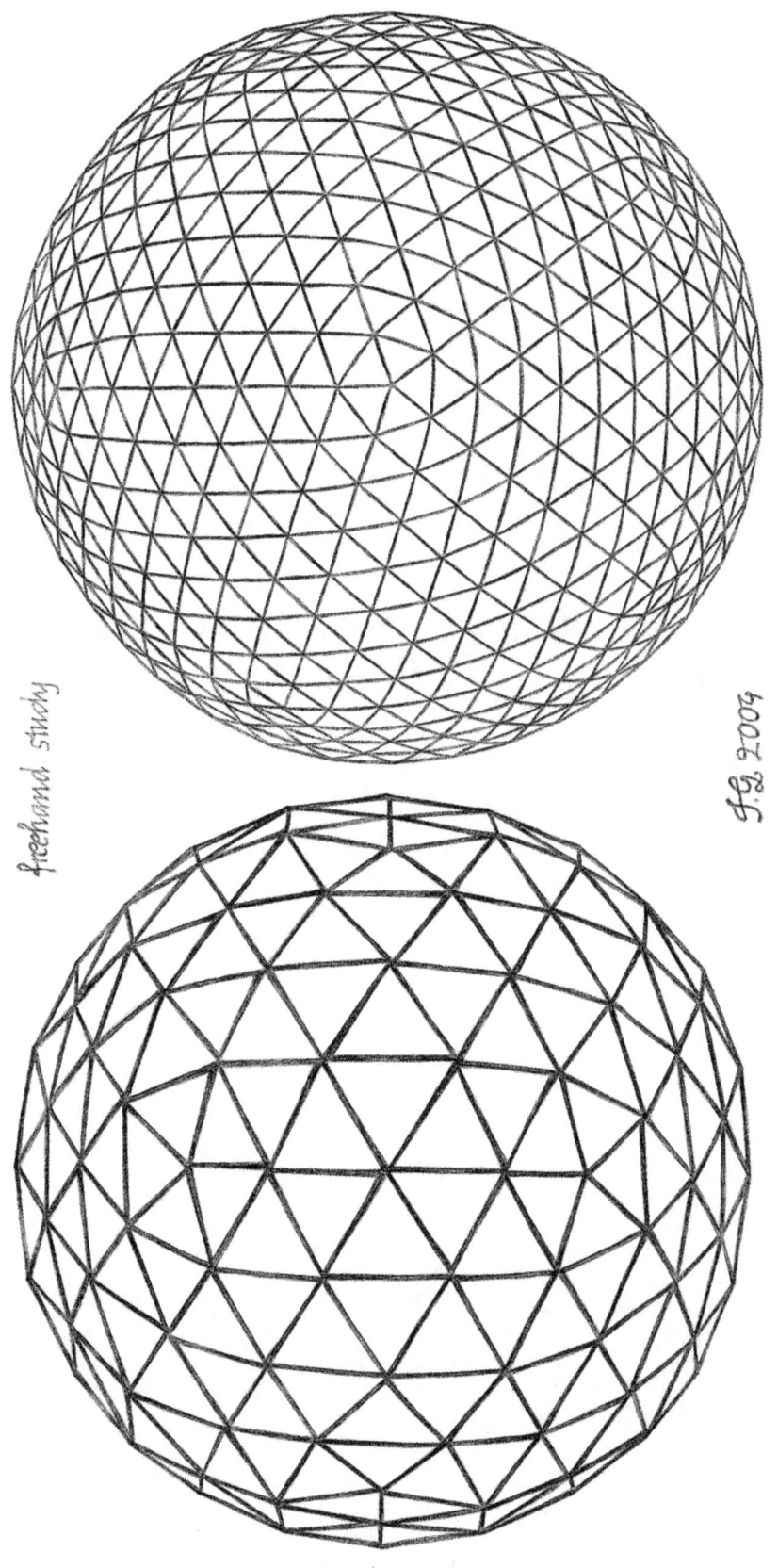

A sphere cannot divide into congruent geometric parts with equal spaces between intersections. But my right example approaches closer than the earlier variant. I must now discover if this plan will serve to place

freehand study

F.G. 2009

the uprights of my bristly ball & also, if there is a shorter path toward my desire.

No 69 is actually the last of the drawings. Soon after my eye-sight very quickly failed

J. v. G.

PLATE 69

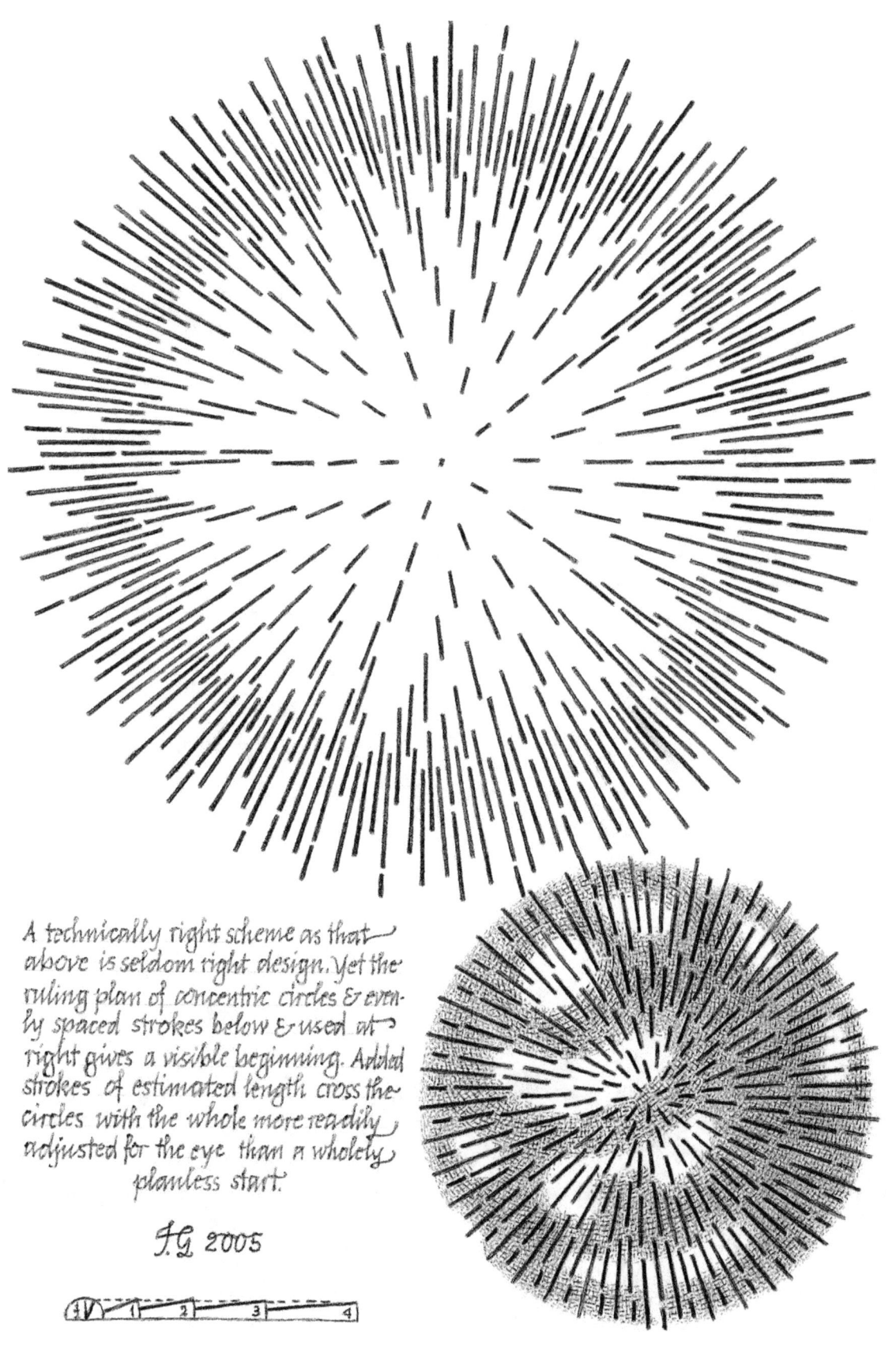

A technically right scheme as that above is seldom right design. Yet the ruling plan of concentric circles & evenly spaced strokes below & used at right gives a visible beginning. Added strokes of estimated length cross the circles with the whole more readily adjusted for the eye than a wholely planless start.

J.G. 2005

PLATE 70

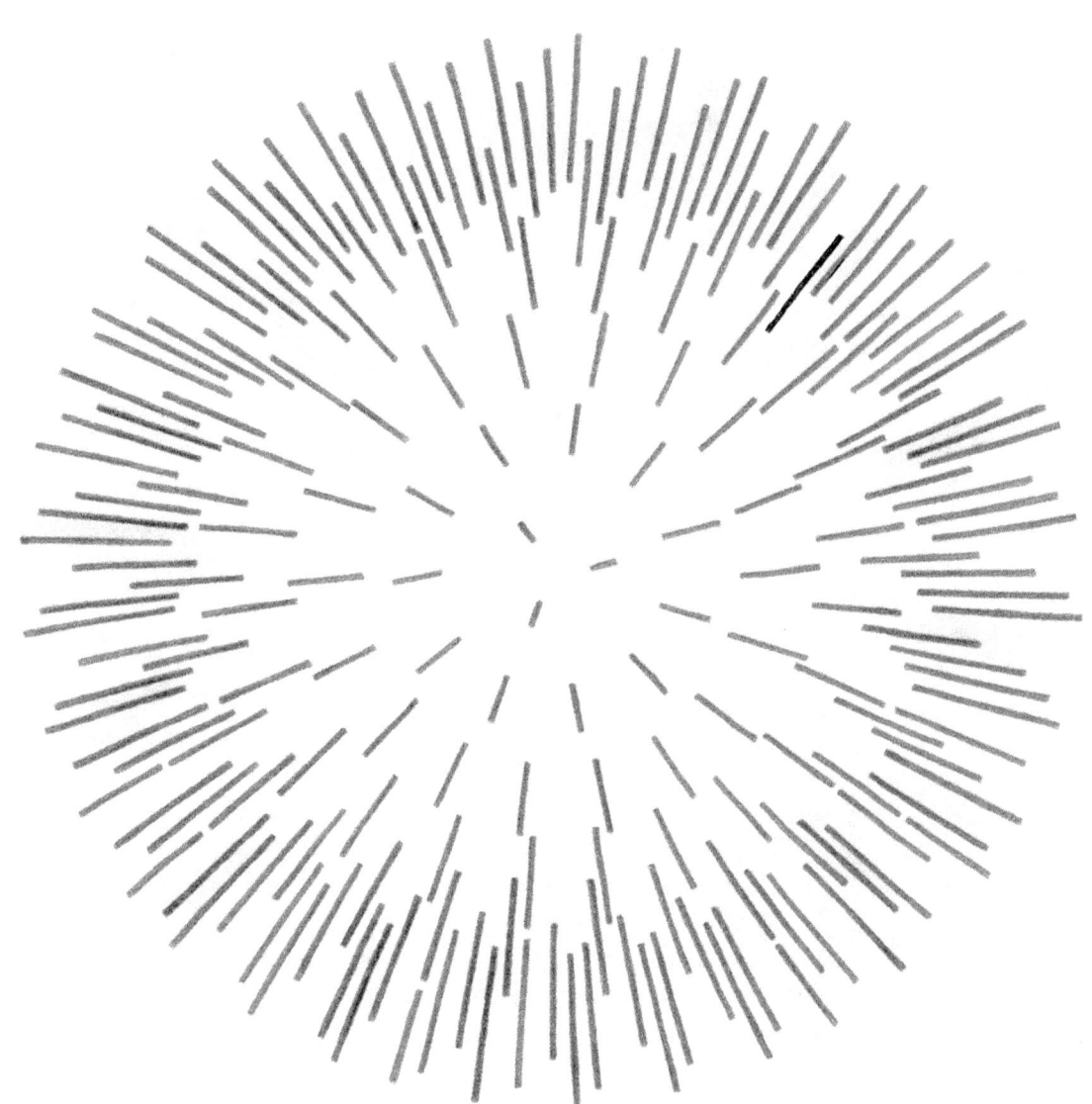

PLATE 71

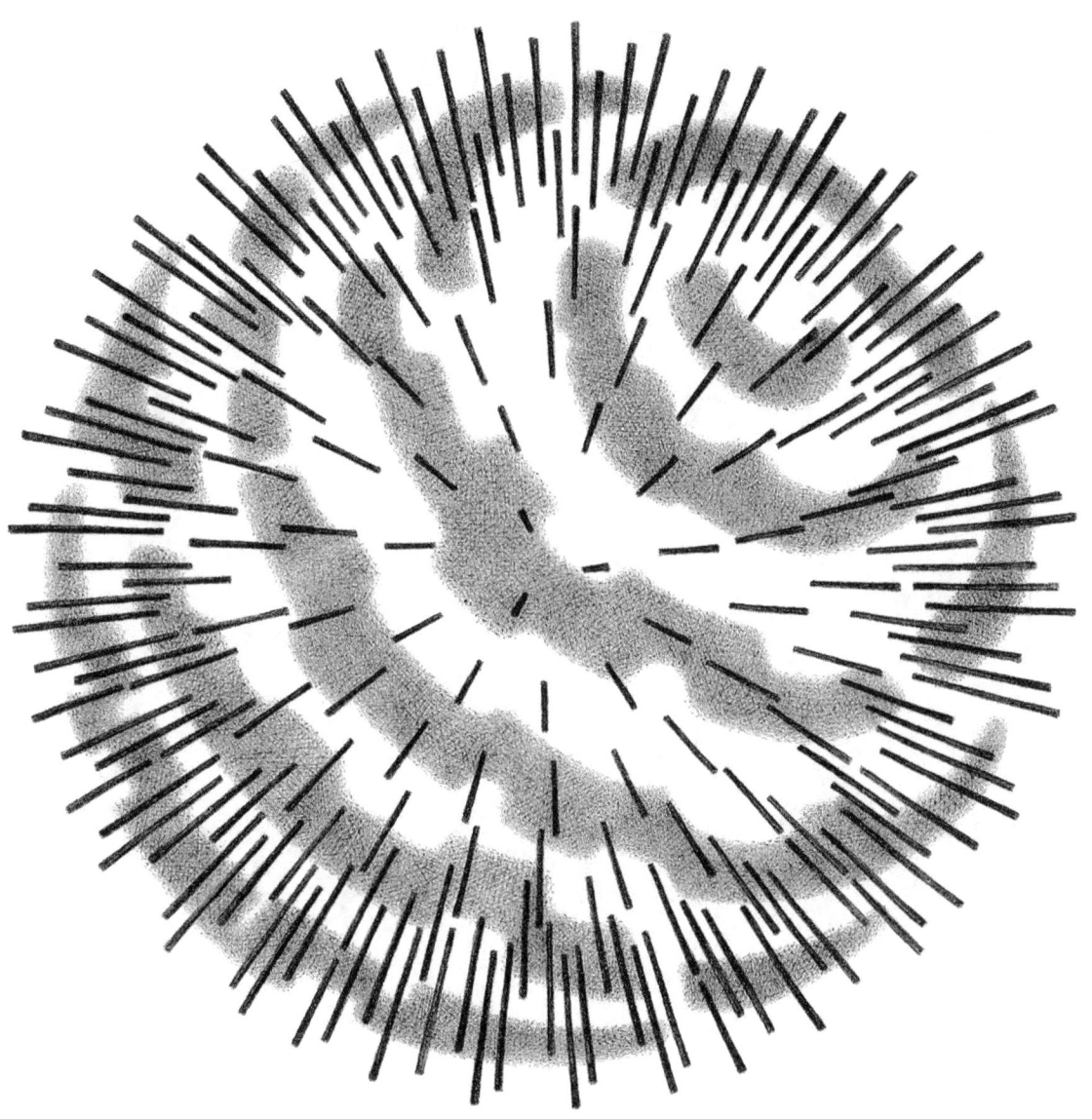

So far as I can tell, we may put observations to two uses: One lies in the particularities of shape & color play — the unrepeatable & varied splendor of a unique relation of light to an array on which it falls.

The second reminds the viewer of observations he has stored within his mind, helping him to recognize a visually rendered object which resembles but is not the same as those which earlier have instructed him in nature.

Of more than half a dozen observations, I employ here the increasing density & length of the bristles outward & let them seemingly arise off the surface of the sphere. That arising is product of mostly slender & uneven fields of tone which, through describing roundness, show us volume & through open spaces repeatedly allow details of the texture to come through.

In this way, features observed in one place, by proving useful in related cases, can stimulate repeatable associations & constitute thereby fundamental lore.                    J.G. 2004

PLATE 72

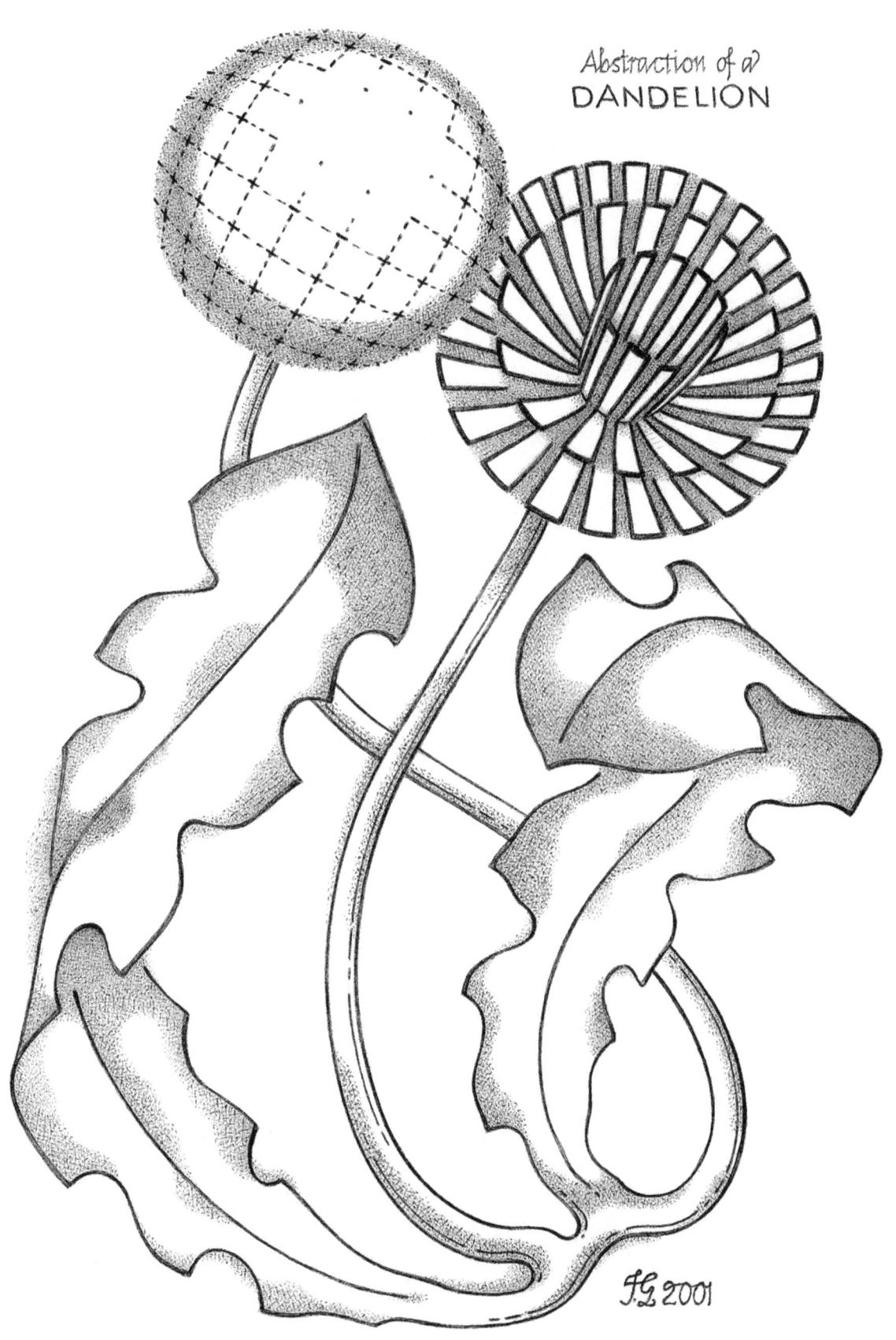

Abstraction of a
DANDELION

*PLATE 73*

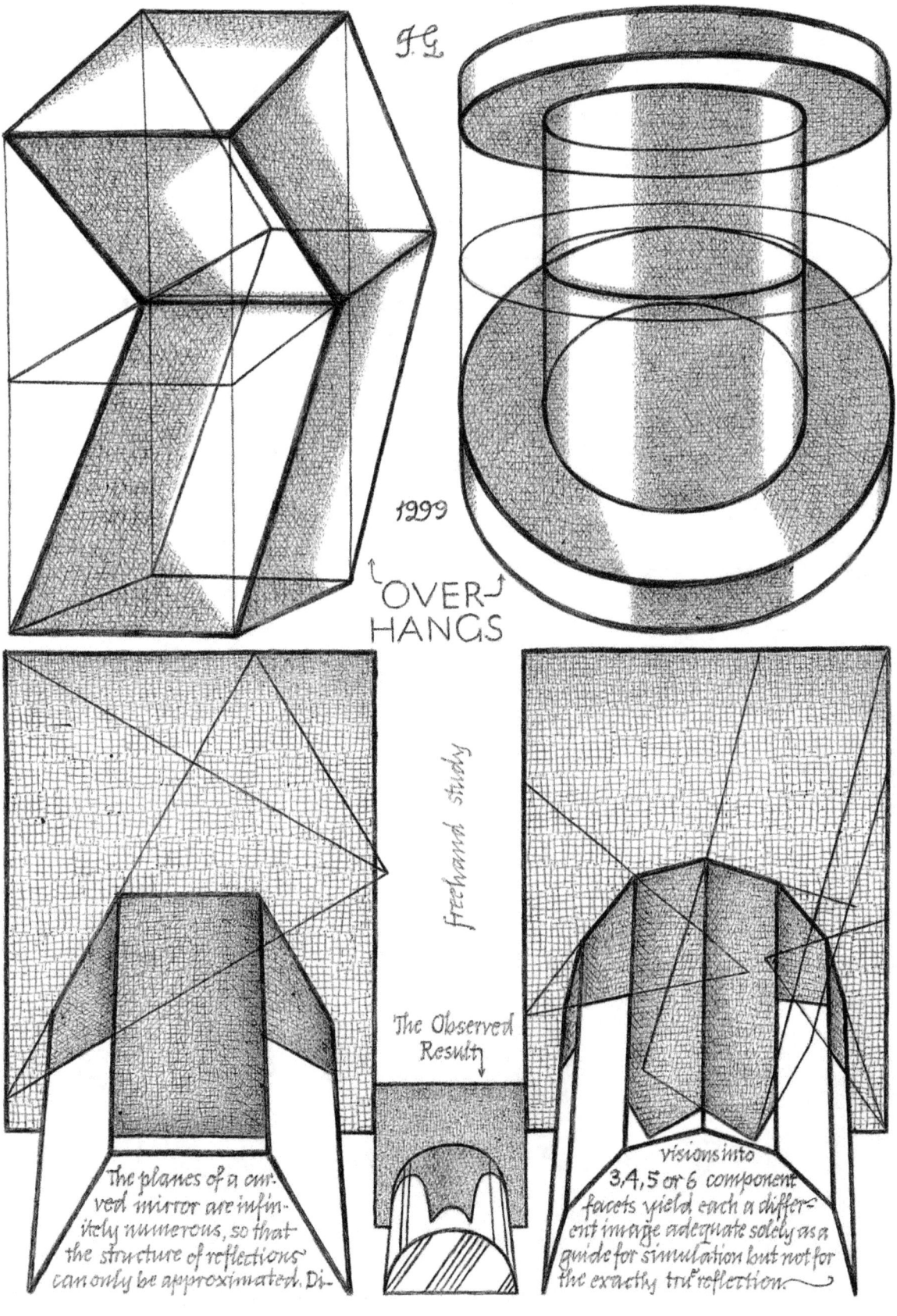

F.G.

1999

OVER-
HANGS

freehand study

The Observed
Result ↓

The planes of a cur-
ved mirror are infin-
itely numerous, so that
the structure of reflections
can only be approximated. Di-

visions into
3, 4, 5 or 6 component
facets yield each a different image adequate solely as a
guide for simulation but not for
the exactly true reflection.

PLATE 74

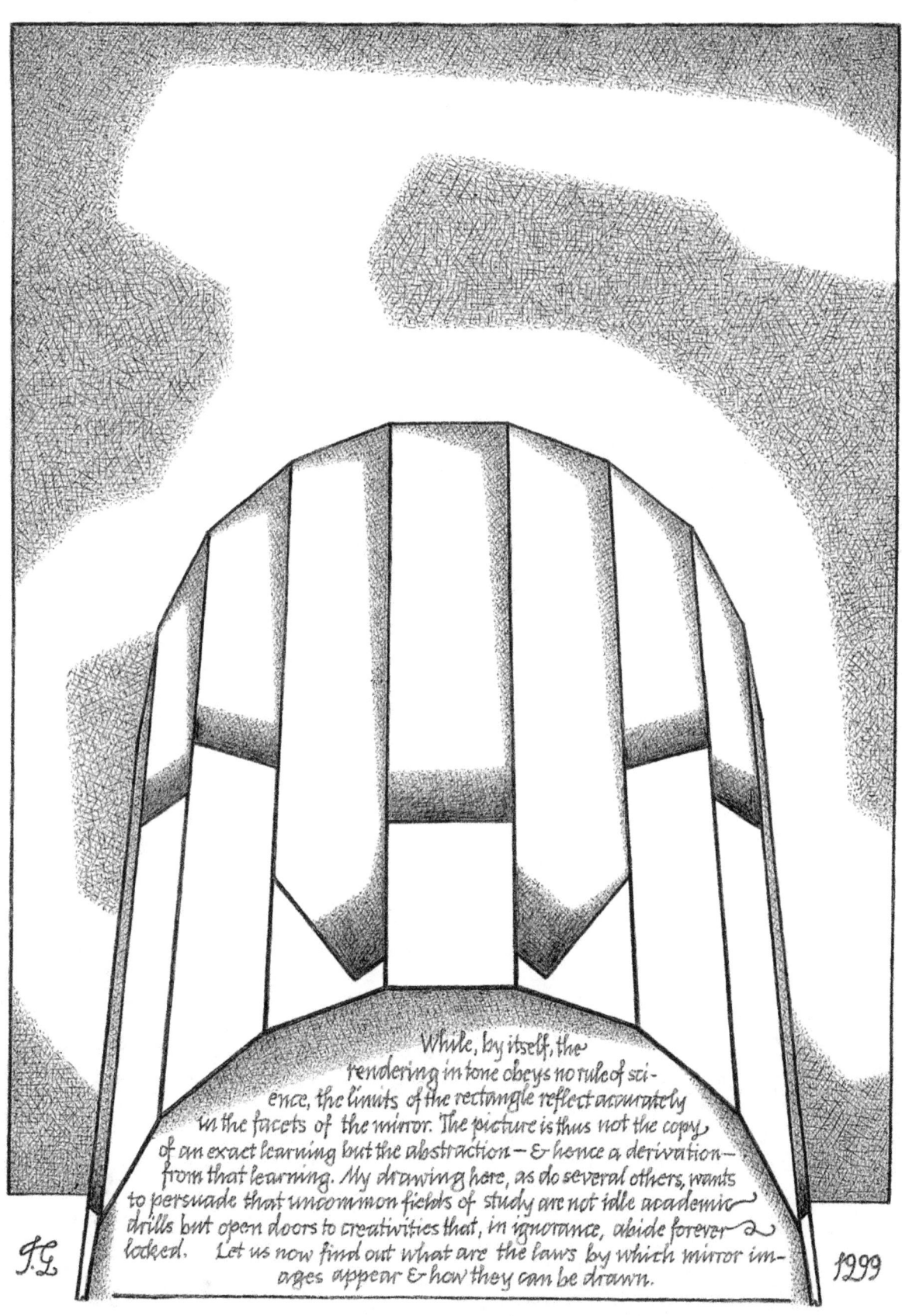

While, by itself, the rendering in tone obeys no rule of science, the limits of the rectangle reflect accurately in the facets of the mirror. The picture is thus not the copy of an exact learning but the abstraction — & hence a derivation — from that learning. My drawing here, as do several others, wants to persuade that uncommon fields of study are not idle academic drills but open doors to creativities that, in ignorance, abide forever locked. Let us now find out what are the laws by which mirror images appear & how they can be drawn.

1999

*PLATE 75*

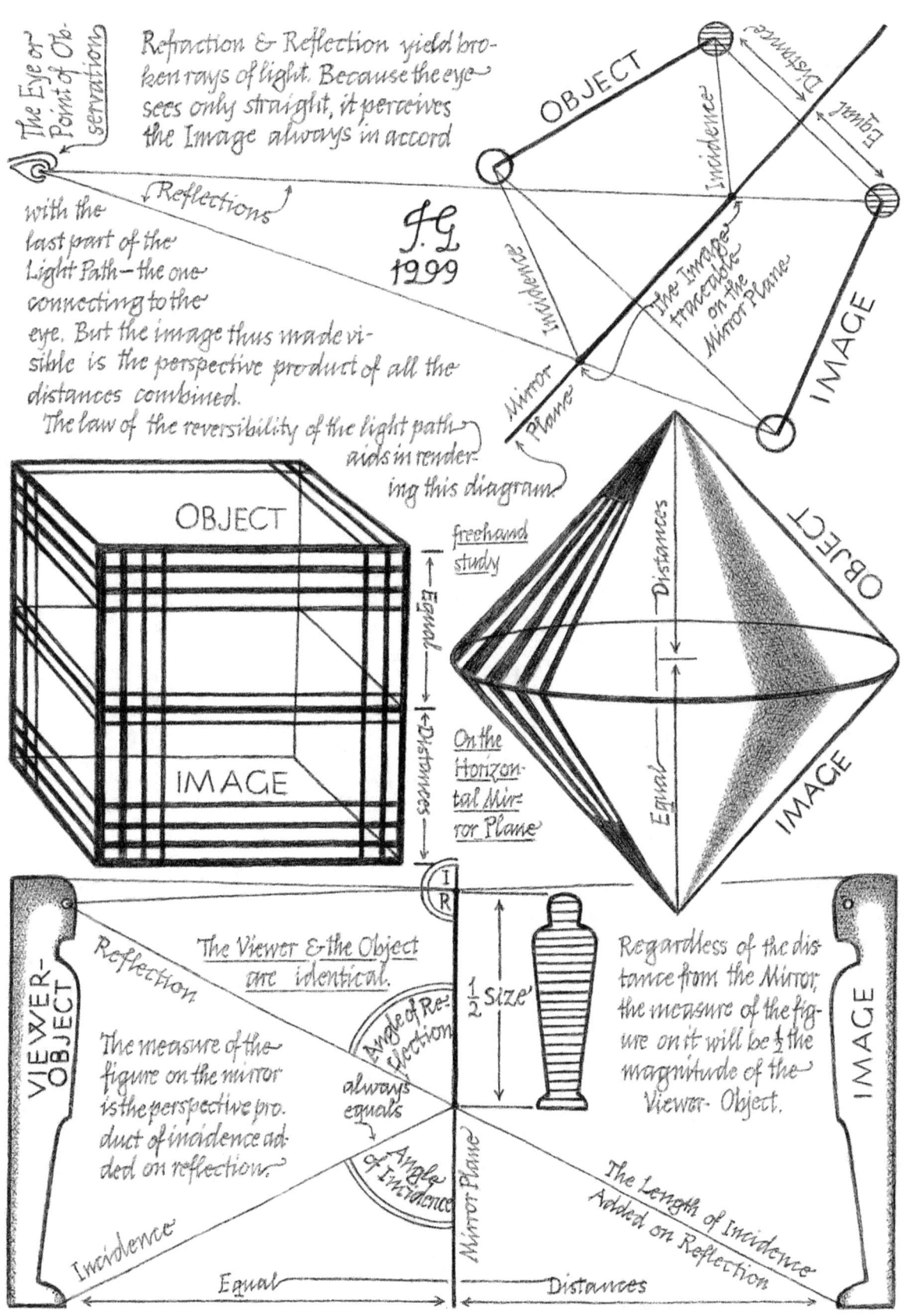

Refraction & Reflection yield broken rays of light. Because the eye sees only straight, it perceives the Image always in accord with the last part of the Light Path—the one connecting to the eye. But the image thus made visible is the perspective product of all the distances combined.

The law of the reversibility of the light path aids in rendering this diagram.

The Eye or Point of Observation

Reflections

J.G. 1999

OBJECT — IMAGE — Incidence — Distance — Equal — Mirror Plane — The Image traceable on the Mirror Plane

OBJECT — IMAGE — Equal — Distances

freehand study

On the Horizontal Mirror Plane

Distances — Equal — OBJECT — IMAGE

VIEWER-OBJECT — Reflection — The Viewer & the Object are identical.

The measure of the figure on the mirror is the perspective product of incidence added on reflection.

Incidence — Angle of Reflection — always equals — Angle of Incidence — Mirror Plane — ½ Size'

Regardless of the distance from the Mirror, the measure of the figure on it will be ½ the magnitude of the Viewer-Object.

IMAGE — The Length of Incidence Added on Reflection — Equal — Distances — I/R

PLATE 76

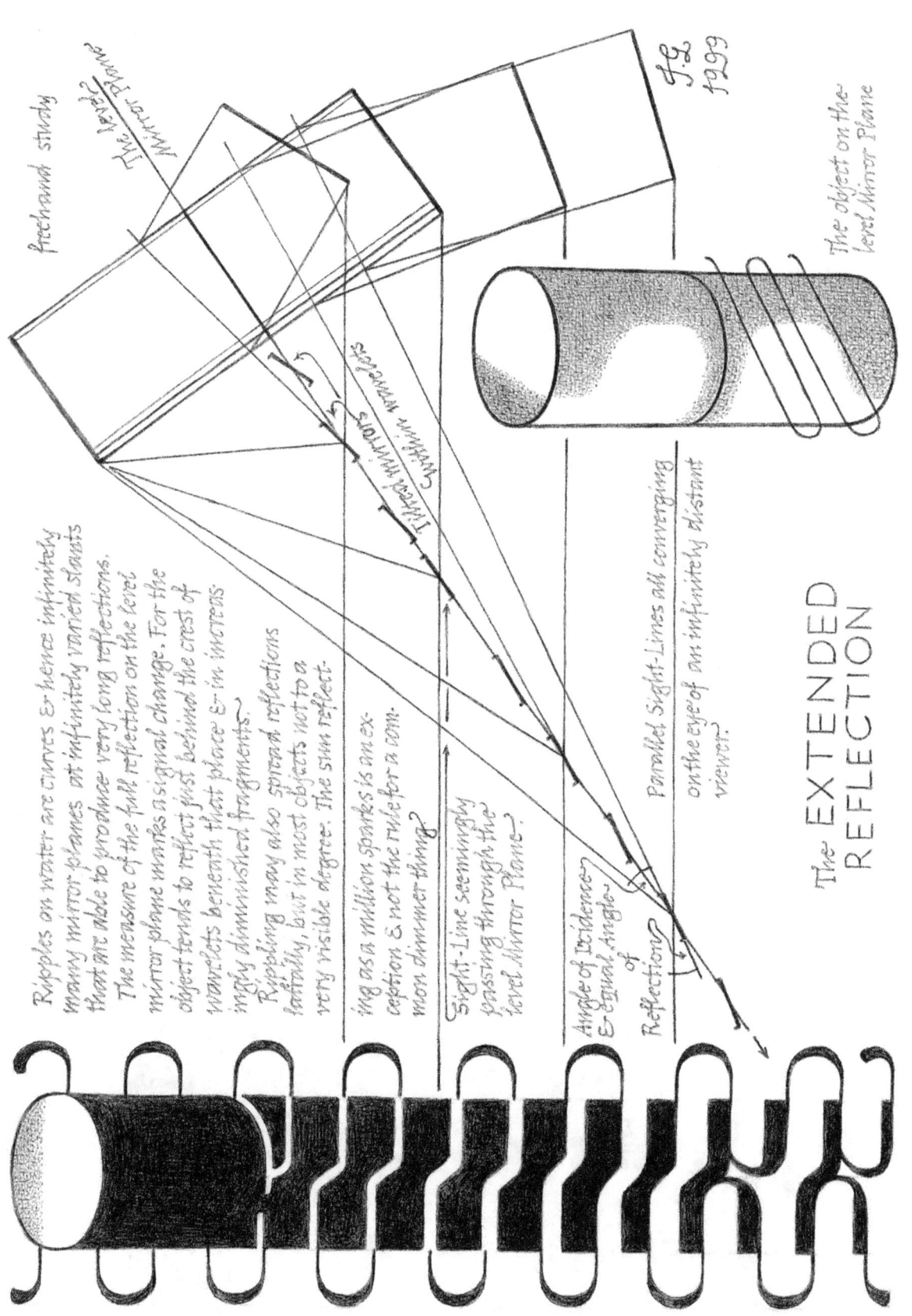

freehand study

The Level Mirror Plane

J.L. 1999

The object on the level Mirror Plane

Ripples on water are curves & hence infinitely many mirror planes at infinitely varied slants that are able to produce very long reflections. The measure of the full reflection on the level mirror plane marks a signal change. For the object tends to reflect just behind the crest of wavelets beneath that place & in waters imply diminished fragments.

Rippling may also spread reflections laterally, but in most objects not to a very visible degree. The sun reflect-

ing as a million sparks is an ex- ception & not the rule for a com- mon dimmer thing?

Tilted mirrors within wavelets

Sight-Line seemingly passing through the level Mirror Plane.

Angle of Incidence Equal Angle of Reflection.

Parallel Sight-Lines all converging on the eye of an infinitely distant viewer.

The EXTENDED REFLECTION

*PLATE 77*

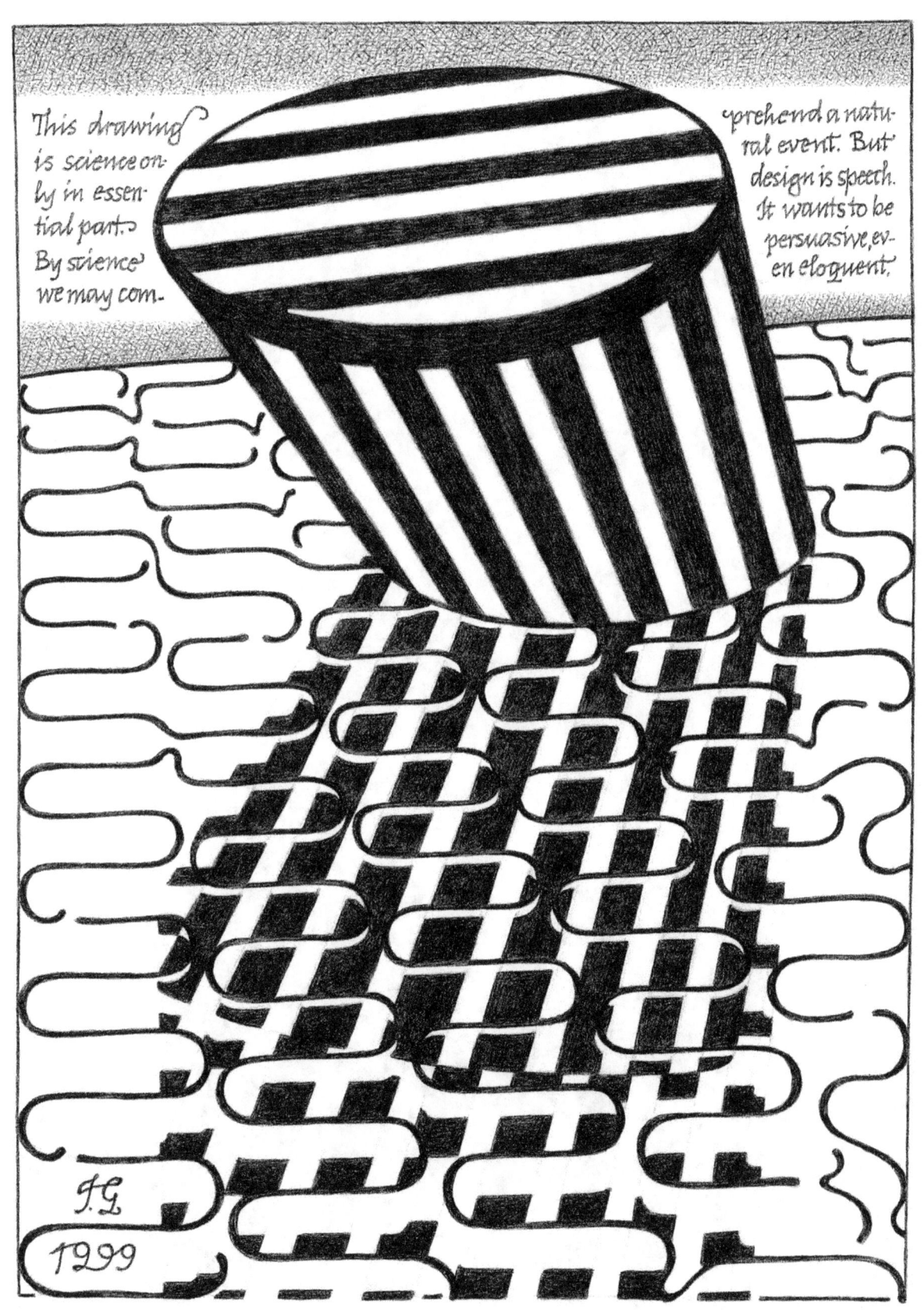

This drawing
is science on-
ly in essen-
tial part.
By science
we may com-

prehend a natu-
ral event. But
design is speech.
It wants to be
persuasive, ev-
en eloquent.

J.G.
1999

*PLATE 78*

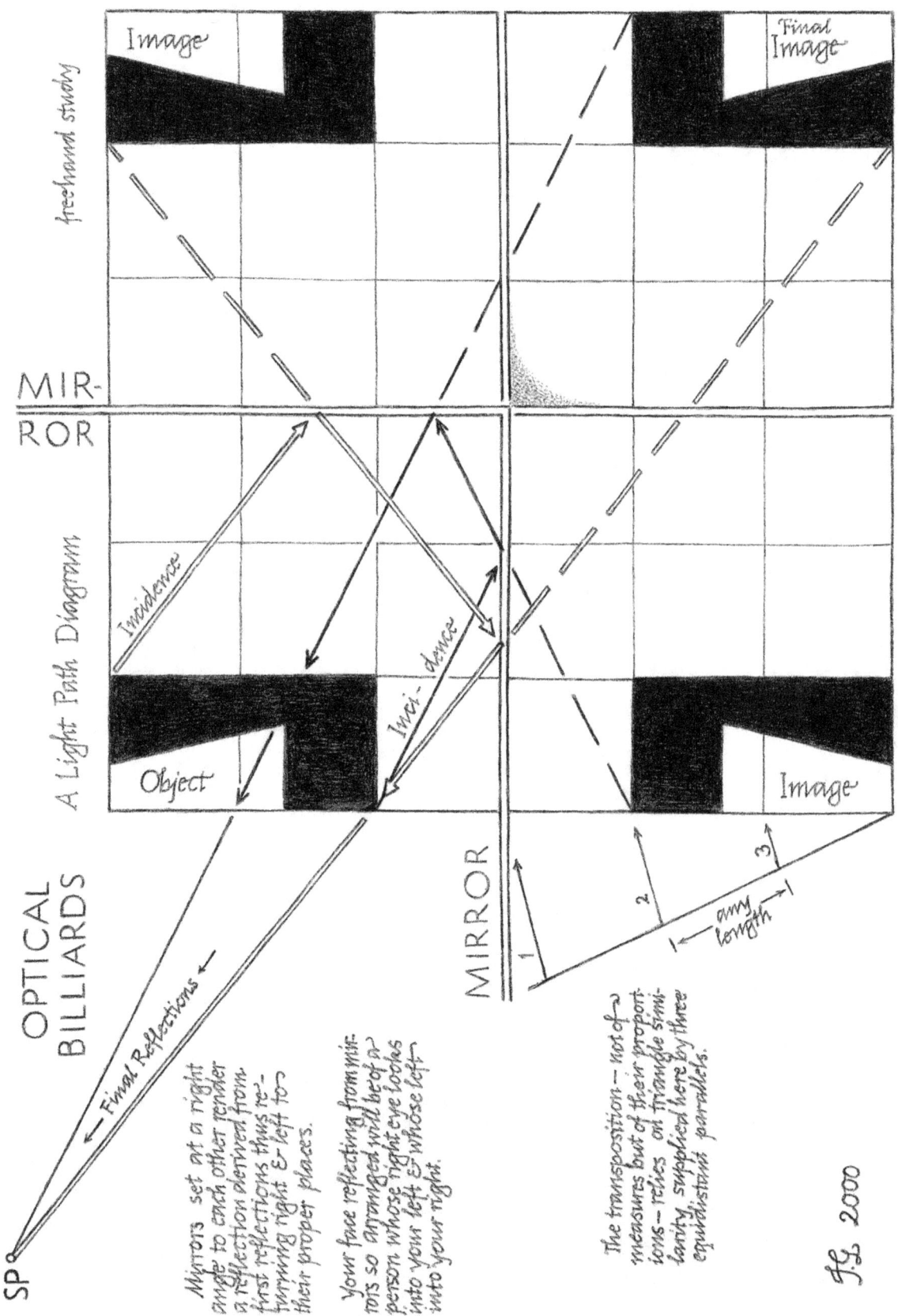

OPTICAL
BILLIARDS

A Light Path Diagram

MIR-
ROR

freehand study

Image

Incidence

Object

Inci-
dence

Image

Final Image

Image

MIRROR

SP

← Final Reflections →

Mirrors set at a right angle to each other render a reflection derived from first reflections thus re-turning right & left to their proper places.

Your face reflecting from mir-rors so arranged will be of a person whose right eye looks into your left & whose left into your right.

1  2  3
← any length →

The transposition — not of measures but of their proport-ions — relies on triangle simi-larity, supplied here by three equidistant parallels.

fL 2000

PLATE 79

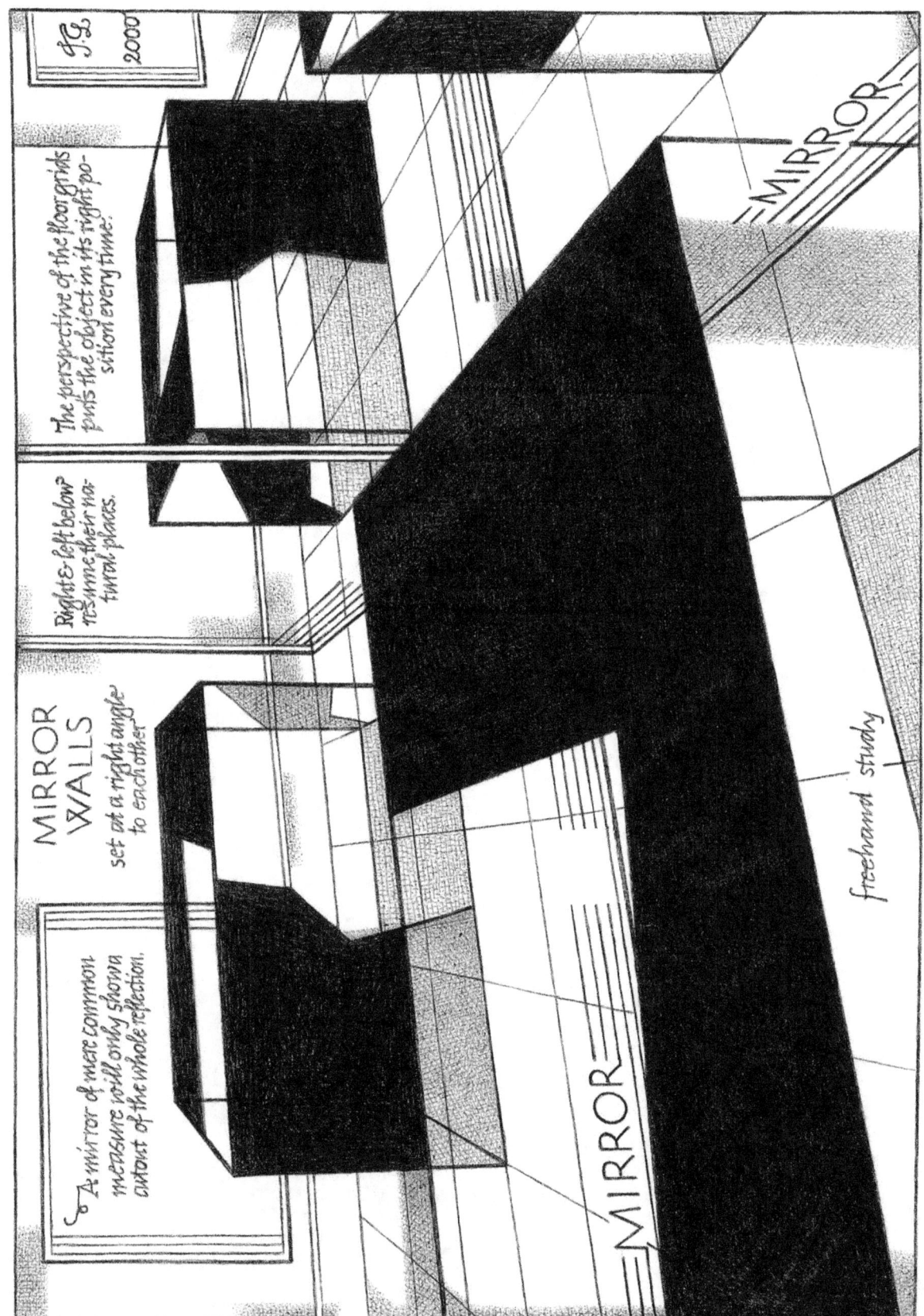

PLATE 80

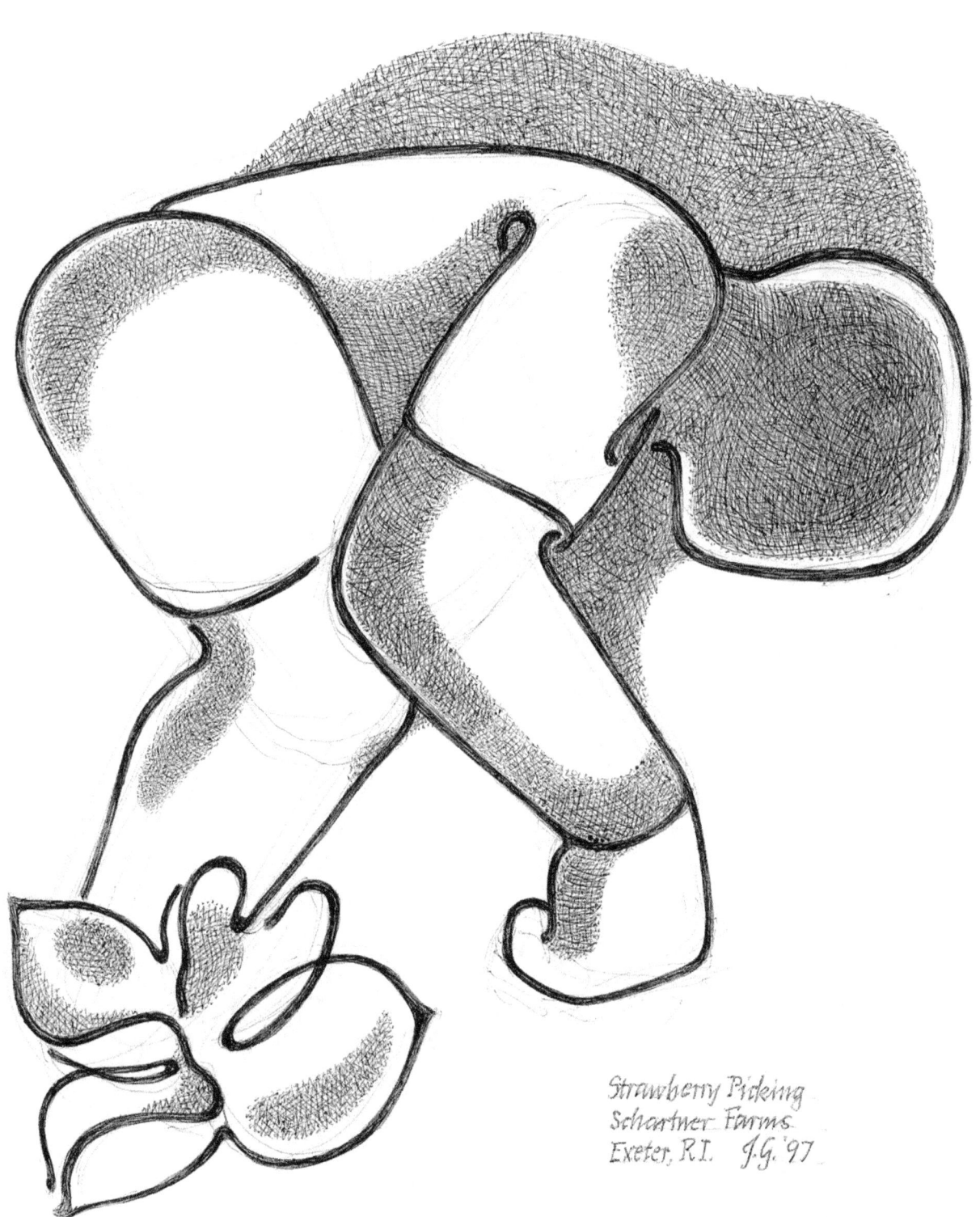

Strawberry Picking
Schartner Farms
Exeter, R.I.    J.G. '97

PLATE 81

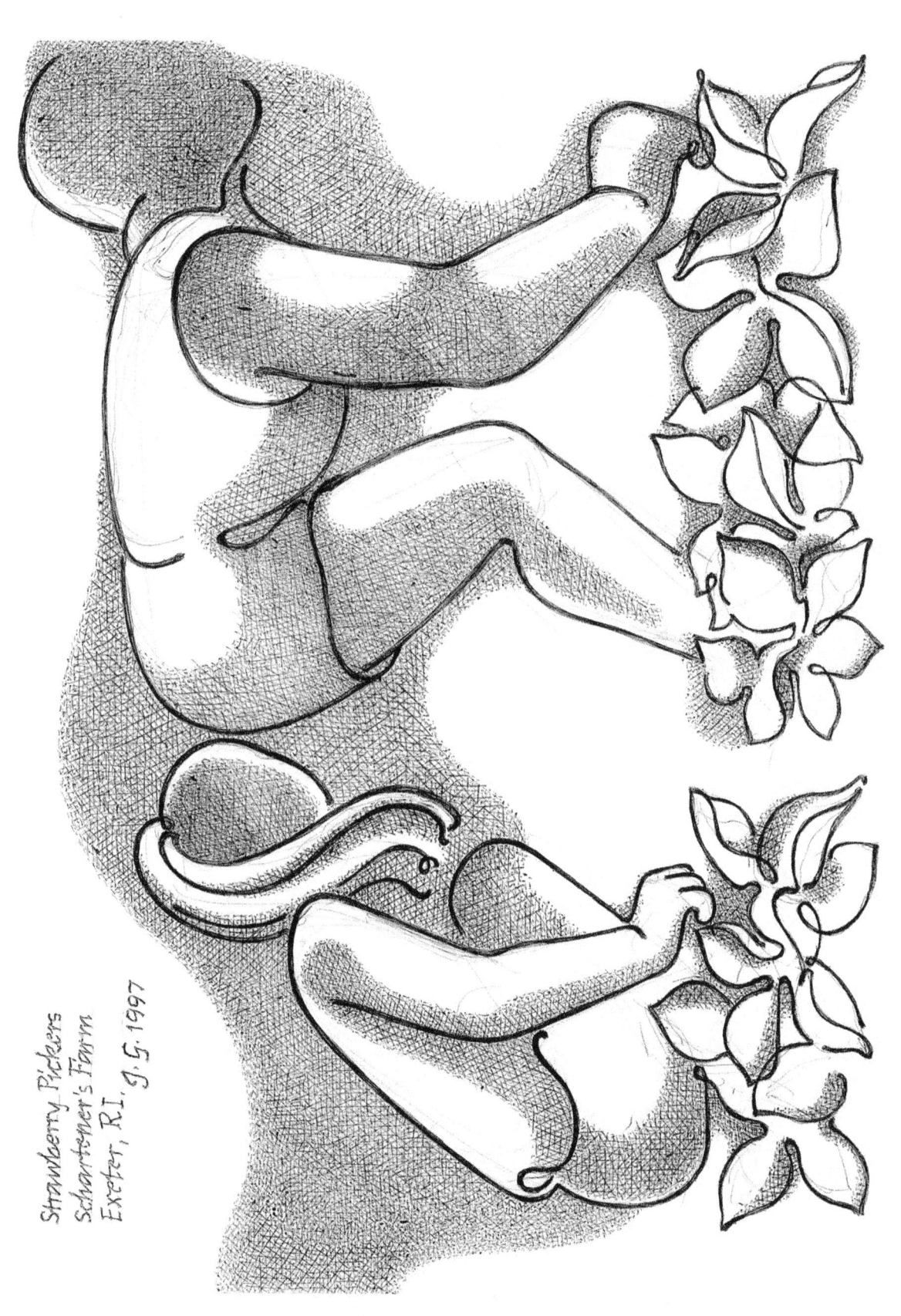

Strawberry Pickers
Schartner's Farm
Exeter, R.I. g.g. 1997

PLATE 82

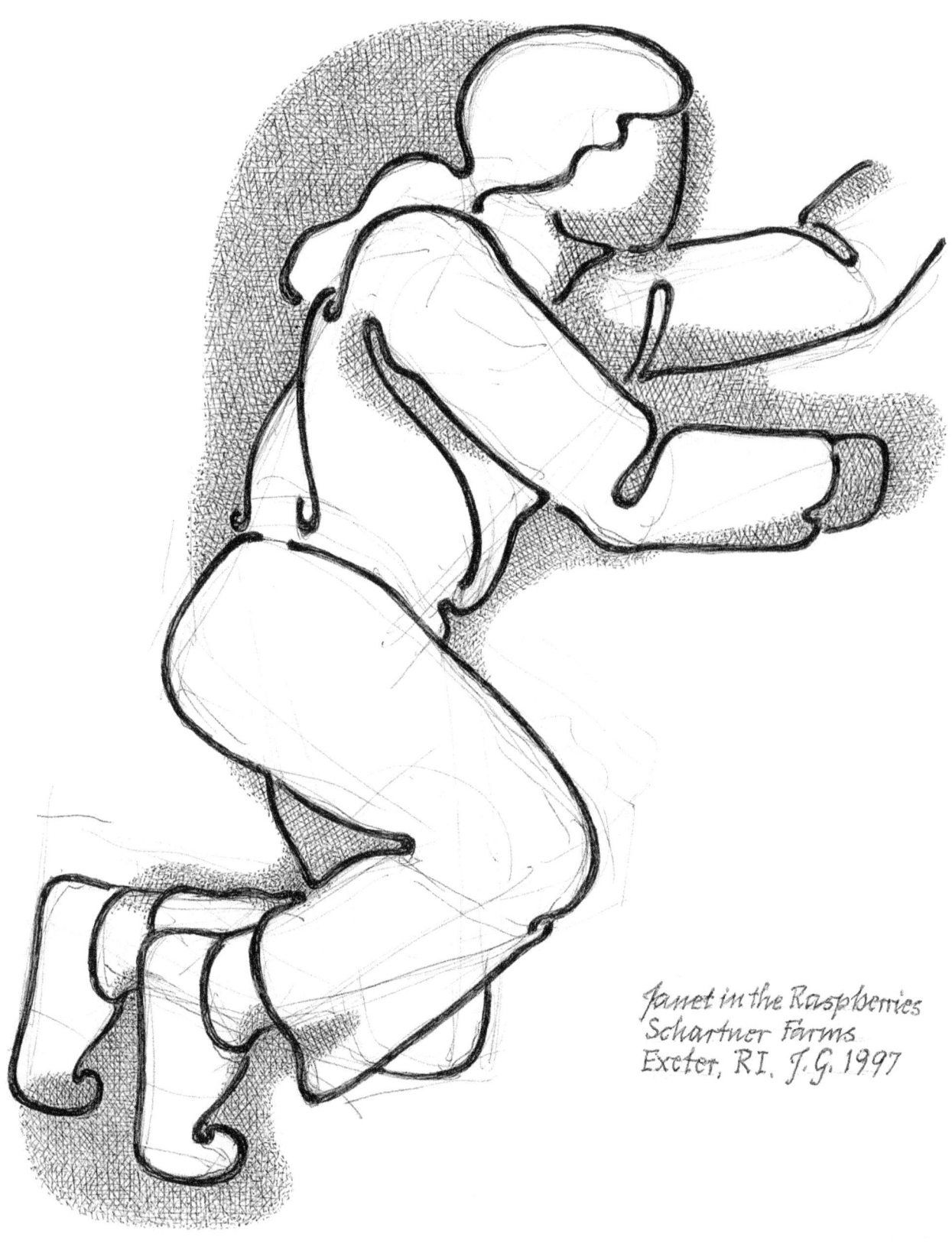

Janet in the Raspberries
Schartner Farms
Exeter, RI. J.G. 1997

PLATE 83

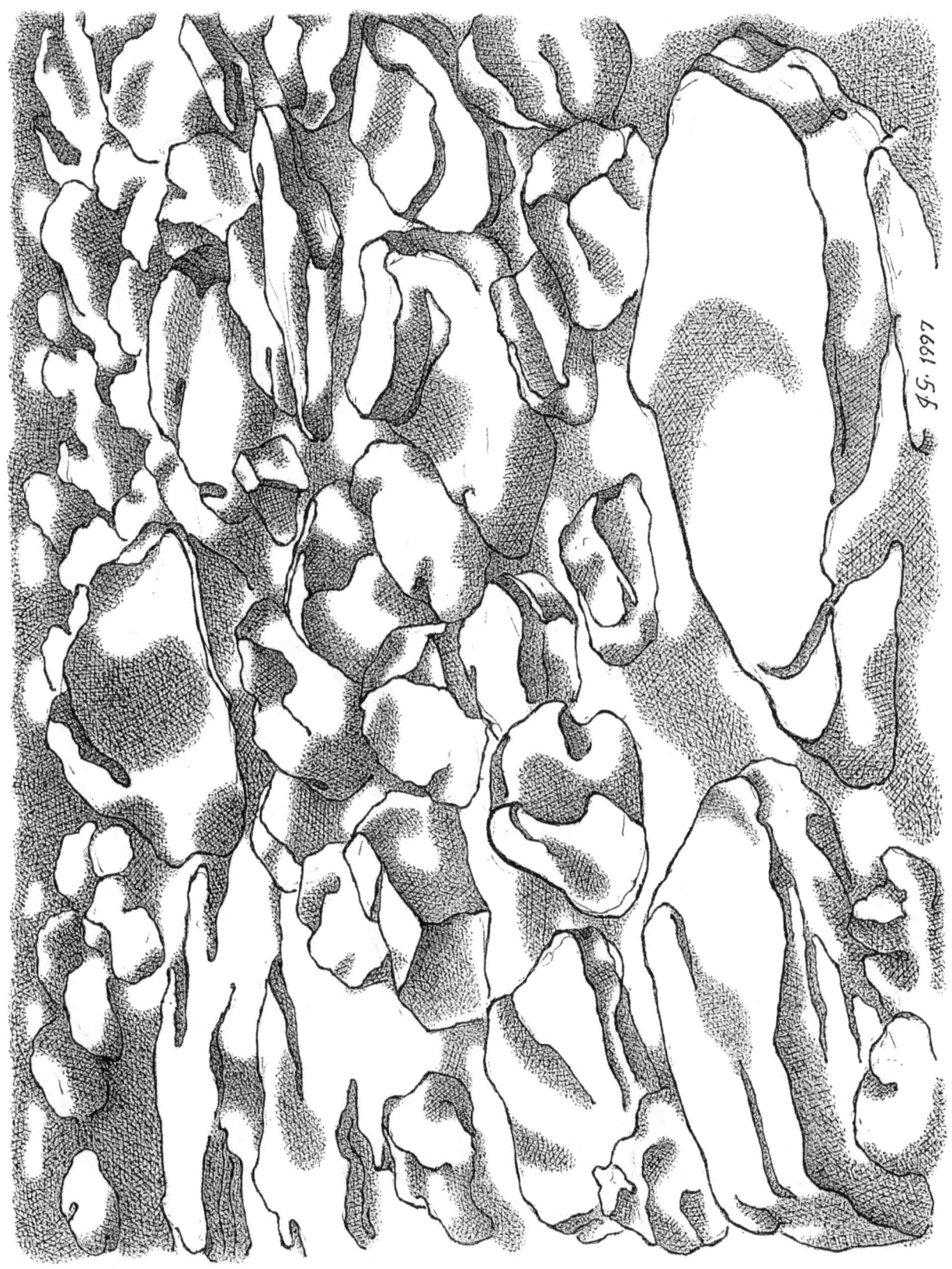

PLATE 84

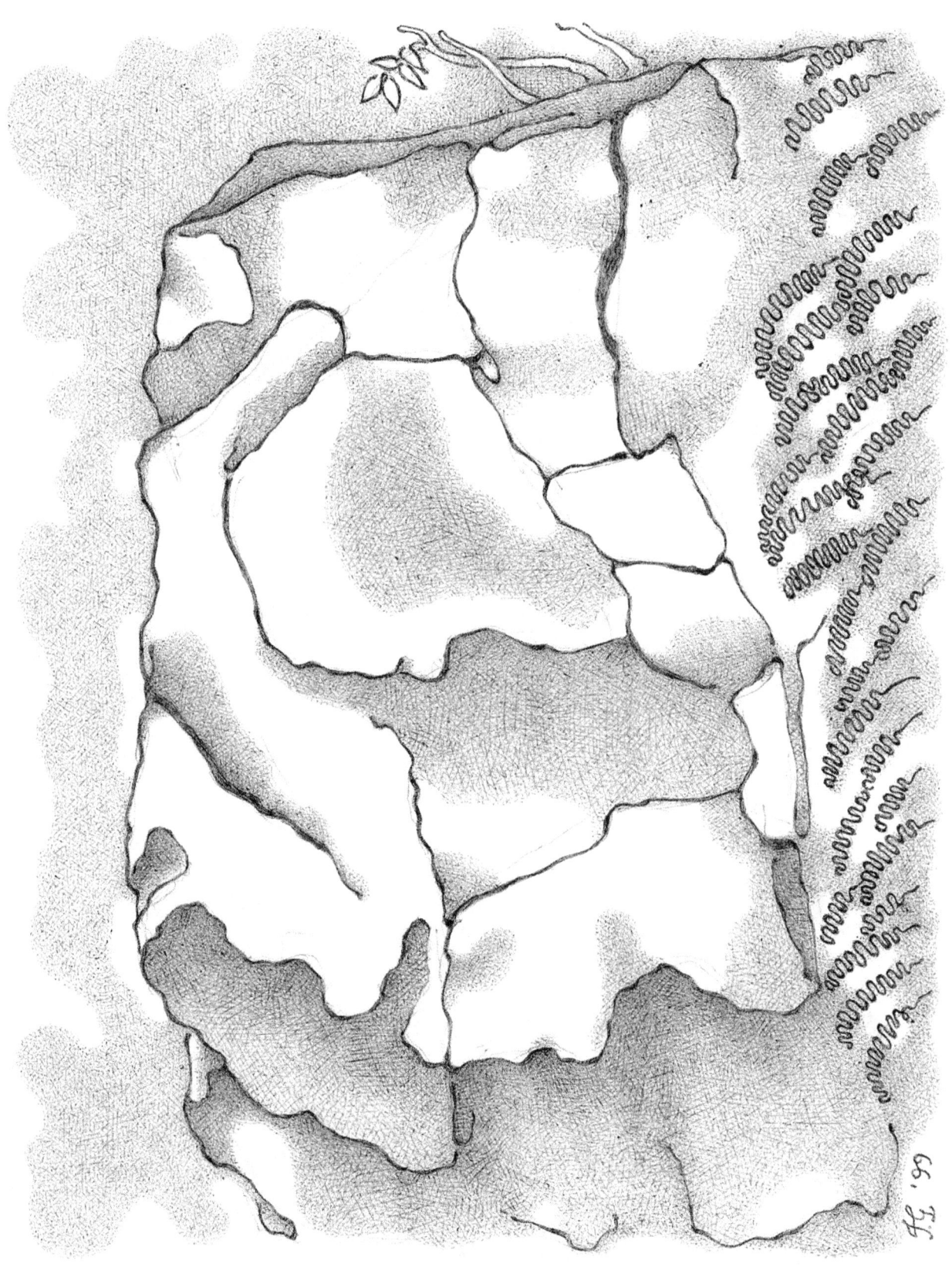

PLATE 85

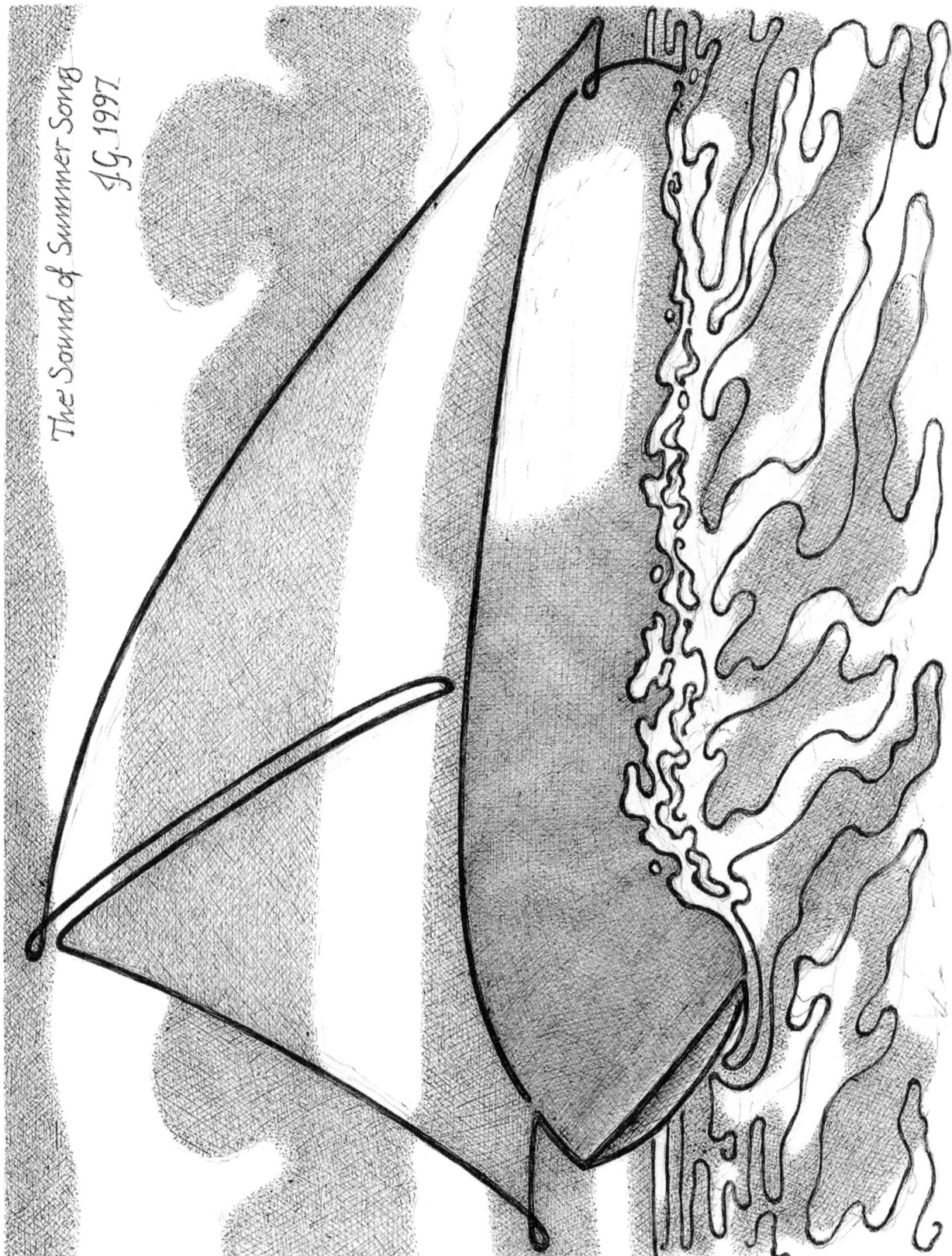

The Sound of Summer Song
J.G. 1997

PLATE 86

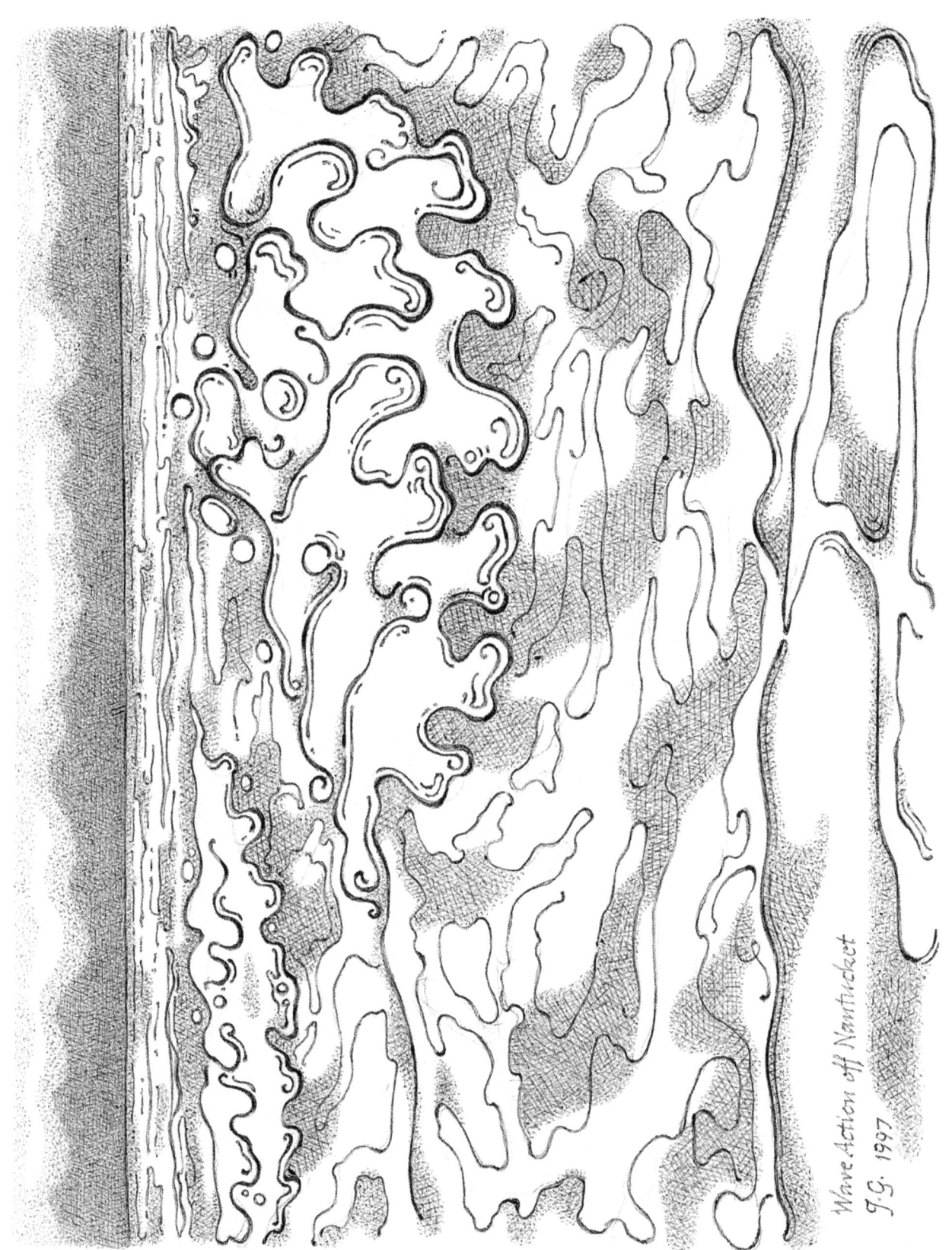

Wave Action off Nantucket
J.G. 1997

PLATE 87

'98

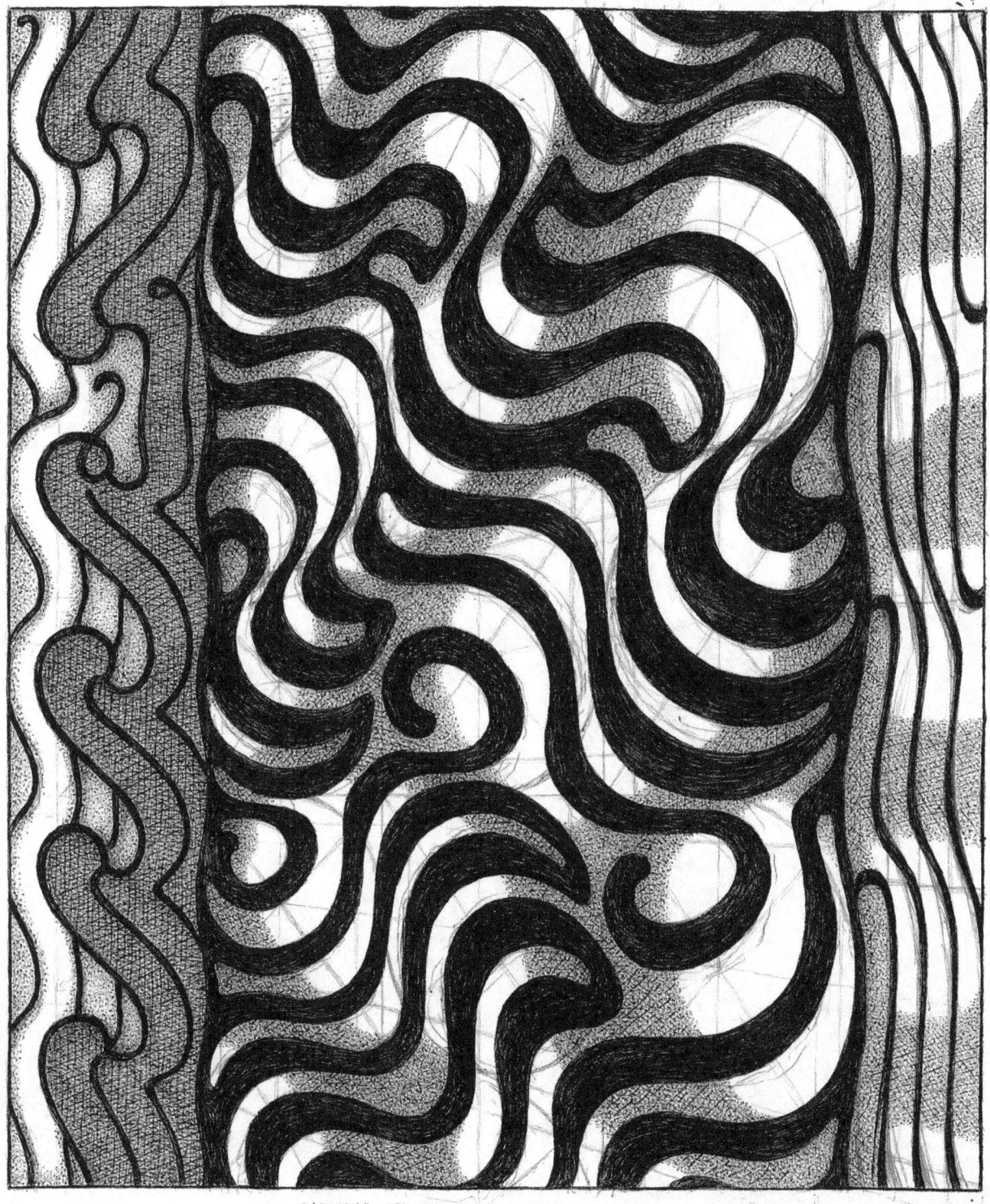

Water, Sand & Clouds

H.L.

PLATE 88

# MIRROR OPTICS, REFRACTION, LIGHT & ⌇

**SHADE** are each a class of study we may, besides delineating them from observation, seek to manage by descriptive geometric means & so invent a work from start to finish. This task of a sphere & mirror image is unsuitably complex to explain. by it the rules that govern light.

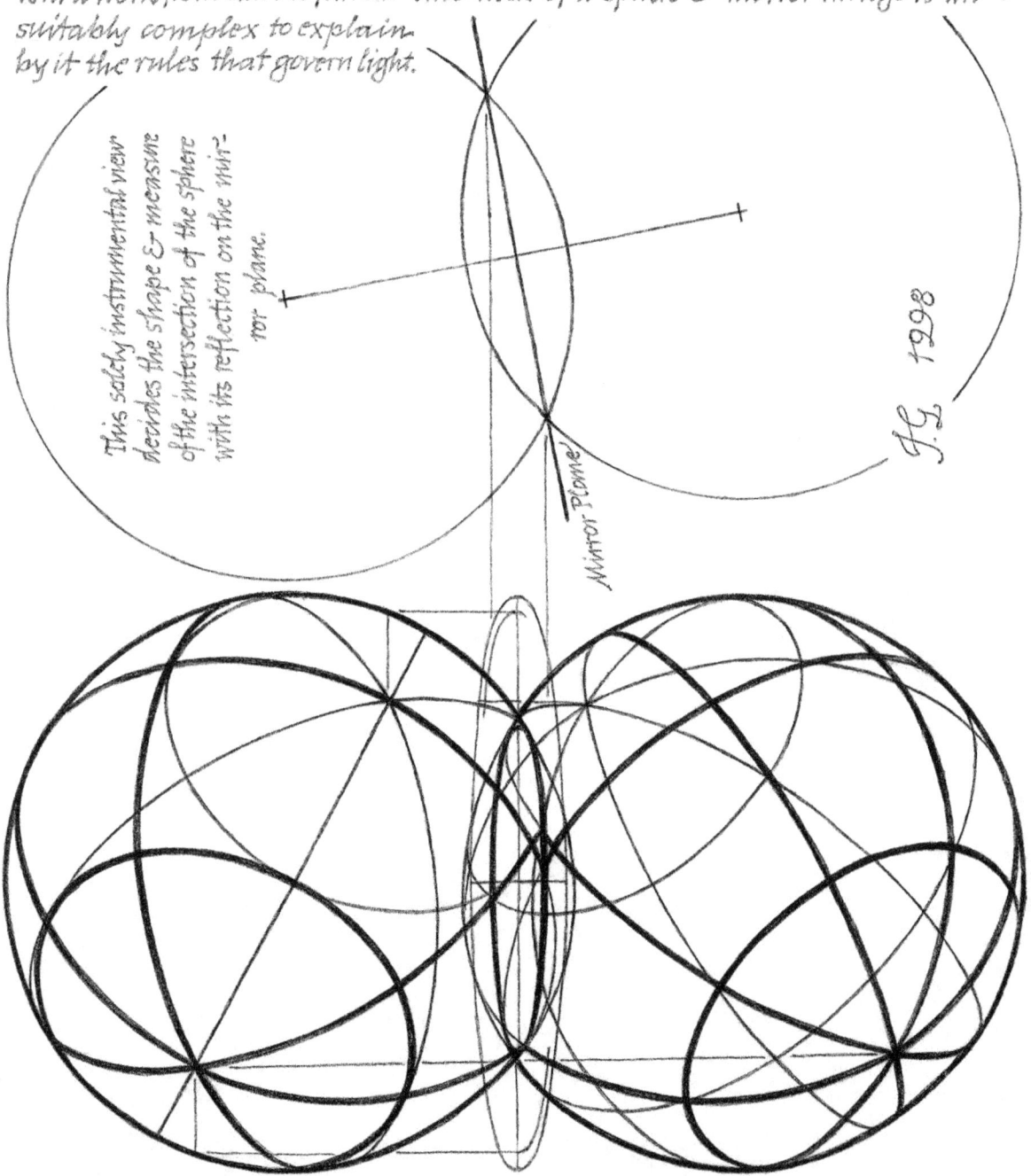

This solely instrumental view decides the shape & measure of the intersection of the sphere with its reflection on the mirror plane.

Mirror plane

J.L. 1998

Yet, once those rules, through easier demonstrations & assignments, have been learned, many such considerable difficulties can be mastered.

*freehand study*

PLATE 89

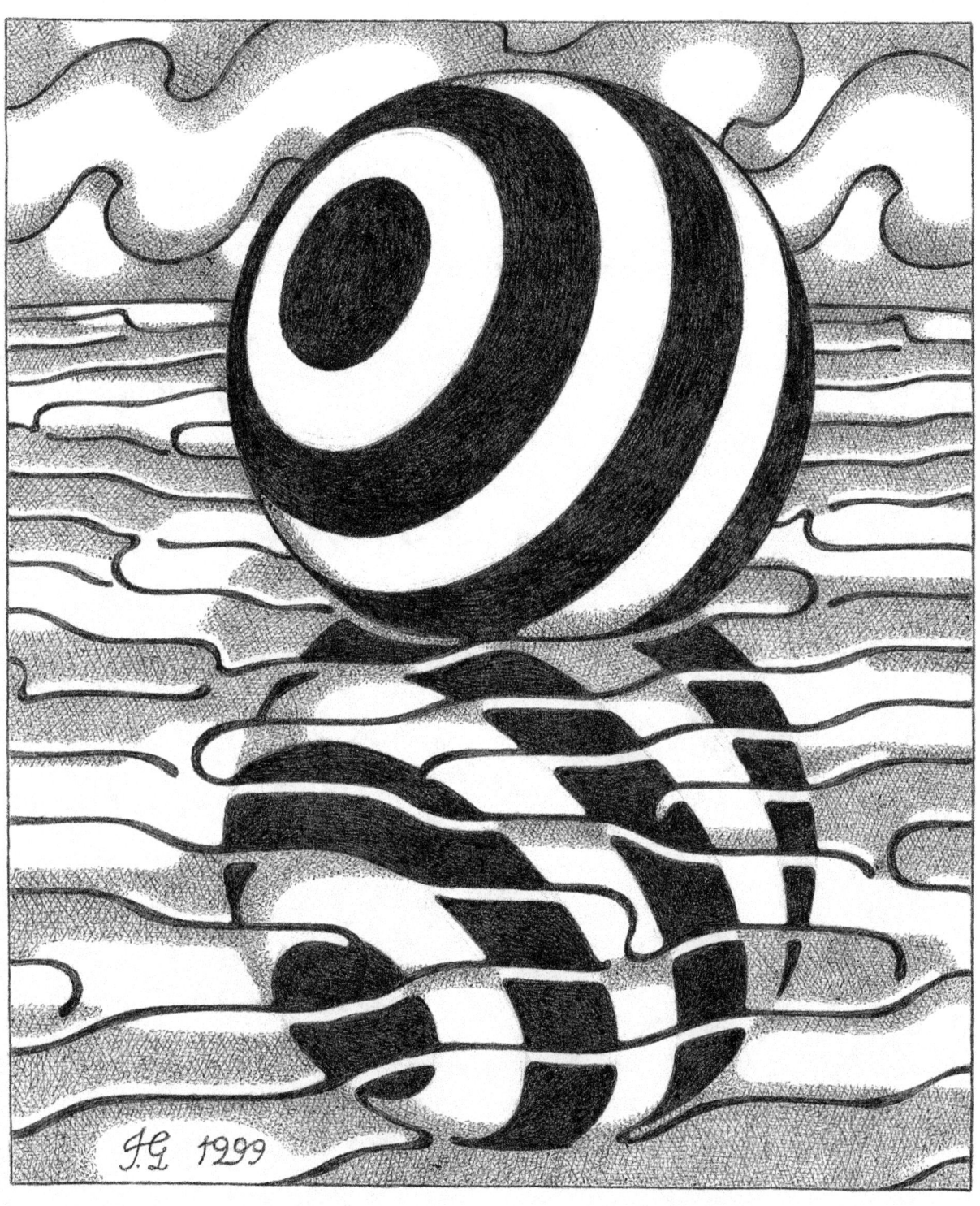